THE
MAURICE MOORE-BETTY
COOKING SCHOOL
BOOK
OF
FINE COOKING

Also by Maurice Moore-Betty

COOKING FOR OCCASIONS

THE
MAURICE MOORE-BETTY
COOKING SCHOOL
BOOK
OF
FINE COOKING

by

MAURICE MOORE-BETTY

ARBOR HOUSE

New York

To my students, past, present and future—
May they cook with a light hand and a lighter heart.

❧ CONTENTS ❧

INTRODUCTION

WINTER

SPRING

SUMMER

CONTENTS

AUTUMN

THE YEAR'S END

INDEX

⚜ INTRODUCTION ⚜

When I first arrived in the United States, new acquaintances would remark, "Oh, so you're a gourmet cook!" At first I thought they were under the impression that I was an exponent of a new method of cooking using ingredients known to a chosen few. I hastily explained that I was nothing more exalted than a person with a life-long interest in and exposure to good food and a deeply held ambition to make accessible the art of cooking as I saw it in its purest form. And further, that there were in my life three kinds of food only, bad food, good food and very haute cuisine, for which an entire day might easily be given up to the preparation of a single dish.

It took some time for me to learn that my United States friends' understanding of the word "gourmet" assumed the use of a glass of red wine, a clove of garlic or herb of reasonable unfamiliarity in cooking to be the dividing line between dishes for everyday eating and those for special occasions with the object of impressing one's guests. It was almost inconceivable to my acquaintances that these simple commodities were in everyday use in many ordinary kitchens throughout Europe.

It was then, I think, that I discovered a great desire to teach, which continued until two years later when I established a school for cooking, now nine years ago. I vowed to myself to teach anyone willing and able the methods and styles that I had been fortunate enough to learn from M. Avignon of London's Ritz Hotel. This, with my life's knowledge of good food, gave me, I thought, the necessary qualifications.

My first objective with my students is always to break down their fear and to demonstrate that witchcraft and alchemy have no place in the kitchen. Cooking is simply a matter of application, patience and common sense. Although some people are blessed with innate good taste and style, any reasonably intelligent person can acquire the ability to make even the most everyday dish look and taste as if it had come from the kitchen of a maestro. To be creative is a great advantage when it comes to cooking, but any diligent and attentive student can, with encouragement, gain the confidence to be a good and perhaps an excellent cook.

The way to approach the menus in this book is to read very carefully through the introductory notes and through the recipes, then to decide on the organization of the marketing and preparation of the meal. Most of the menus included in this volume may be put together in easy stages. Often one or more of the dishes may be cooked ahead and frozen and others prepared the day before, leaving a very manageable amount of work to be done just before the meal and freeing the cook to be properly attentive to his guests.

Once you've gained some confidence in preparing a dish, you will be able to expand your repertory considerably by varying its ingredients, so long as the correct proportions are preserved. But, as also in the event of doubling or tripling a recipe, take great care in the seasoning of the dish, as any changes may have a considerable effect on the amounts of any herbs, spices and other seasonings needed.

And after you have some acquaintance with the contents of the various menus, you will want to formulate your own. A good deal of the business of menu planning is common sense—avoiding too similar sauces or other preparations in a meal, balancing very rich or heavy dishes with simple and light ones, etc. But your imagination may be used to wonderful effect, if you attend particularly to the color, flavor and texture of foods.

A word of warning: don't treat your guests as guinea pigs. Offer them well and truly tried dishes that you feel at home with. And one of my most deeply held principles—don't overload your guests with food. I rarely serve cocktail food before dinner, preferring that my guests come to the table with an edge to their appetites, perhaps sharpened by a glass of dry sherry and an olive or two. I consider it an affront to have people gorge themselves on cheese and the like beforehand. At the table I serve modest portions, as I would much rather serve second helpings than risk dulling people's appetites with plates piled high with food. Finally, whether for a standard meal or a buffet, it is unnecessary to prepare too many dishes. In fact, I consider it blatant bad taste and evidence of insecurity: it shouldn't be necessary to impress your guests. A few well-chosen, well-cooked dishes, beautifully presented, are infinitely preferable to a groaning board of ill-assorted foods.

THE
MAURICE MOORE-BETTY
COOKING SCHOOL
BOOK
OF
FINE COOKING

❄ WINTER ❄

Being of a stubborn nature, I refuse to adopt the current practice of telescoping the many seasons of the year into one. I still carry with me memories of cold blustery days, thick vegetable soups, hearty stews and hot puddings. Food such as this held our ribs together and generated sufficient heat in our bodies to compensate for the lack of it in our houses, and we lived then at such a pace that the calories were burned off before they had time to swathe our frames in fat.

Freezers were unknown in my young days. In the winter months we ate root vegetables that had been lifted from the ground after the first frost and stored in pits blanketed with straw and sealed with earth. We ate the canned soft fruits and vegetables that had been picked in their prime at the height of the summer and either canned or bottled. Fortunately, the entire family was partial to game, which would be hung till light decomposition set in (pheasants were ready to go to the oven when the tail feathers by which they hung could no longer support them, and they fell to the larder floor). Pork would be cured to make bacon, and beef spiced and salted long in advance of its annual appearance at Christmas. Brussels sprouts and cabbages we ate fresh right through the winter, and the autumn apples and pears were stored on racks in a shed we called the apple house to be fetched into our house on the darkest days.

Having thus eaten our way through winter provender, we were glad with the first signs of spring to turn our attention to a different array of foods. This was the rhythm of centuries of almost unchanged devotion to the raising and preparing of food, providing us always with something to look forward to and with memories that were a promise of the coming seasons.

WINTER LUNCHEON

Filet de Porc Sauvage (Marinated Shoulder Butt of Pork)
Broccoli Harlequin
Endive Salad   Fontina
Apricot Pudding with Apricot Sauce

Serves 6 to 8

This recreation of a classic treatment of wild boar is the basis for one of my favorite winter menus, and one so easy to prepare that I invariably find I've allowed more time for it than is needed. It's a fine example of an imaginative use of pork, a wonderfully versatile meat that I find particularly suited to the rigors of winter.

The marketing for this menu may all be done ahead. The pork can be bought the day before it's to be served and refrigerated in its marinade—it will have to be taken out of the refrigerator five or six hours before it's to be cooked. The cauliflower and broccoli for the Broccoli Harlequin may be prepared in the morning and the dish assembled at your convenience (I've done this as far ahead as the evening before with no ill effects). The endive and parsley for the salad may be washed and stored in the refrigerator and the salad's vinaigrette dressing mixed in the morning and set aside without refrigerating.

The cut of pork you want should be identified to the butcher as the cushion or butt, although it's sometimes mistakenly called a filet. You will need two cushions or butts weighing two and a half to three pounds each to serve six or eight people. Have the butcher tie them tightly with string in sausage shape, or do this yourself. You should use a good red wine for the marinade, a Bordeaux or Burgundy that you would not be ashamed to drink.

For the Broccoli Harlequin you will need a small, very white head of cauliflower and two bundles of fresh green broccoli; examine the stalks and leaves of the broccoli closely to make sure they are not withered and dry. If the broccoli needs freshening, cut a slice from the stalk and let it soak in cold water for an hour or two. The water will be taken up through the stalk and will give the vegetable a new lease on life. To provide myself with the bread crumbs called for, I generally save the ends of the French or

17

Italian loaf that would normally be thrown away, allow them to dry out and then put them through a meat grinder or crush them with a rolling pin or empty bottle.

Buy five to six heads of endive (there is no need to refer to it as "Belgian"; almost all our endive is imported from that country). Remove any discolored outer leaves, then store it in a plastic bag in the refrigerator until about two hours before serving time.

Cheese should be bought whenever possible from a store with a large turnover; it will always be better and fresher than from a store in which the perishable types languish until they are forgotten. I find that the Fontina which I've called for here complements the endive beautifully. And in case you intend to drink more red wine, the cheese will clear your palate and allay the sourness in the salad dressing.

Cheeses should always be taken out of the refrigerator several hours before they're to be eaten and allowed to warm to room temperature, since cold cheeses don't get up their full flavor. If the kitchen is dry, I find that covering the cheese with a clean damp cloth prevents the unnecessary loss of moisture. I like to serve it on wood or on a piece of marble. I never serve butter with cheese, but I'm likely to put out good, crunchy French or Italian bread, plain or whole wheat biscuits, or the soft Armenian bread called pita, toasted. I'll often eat a good dessert apple with cheese, a custom identified to me as a child as originating in Yorkshire.

Get together the ingredients for the pudding about two hours before you plan on serving the meal. If you don't have a steamed pudding mold—one with a lid—use a bowl to be covered with waxed paper and foil and tied securely with string, and fitted inside a large pot. Allow a minimum of an hour and a half for steaming the pudding. A word of advice: get the pudding into the pot of boiling water as quickly as possible after the flour and bicarbonate of soda have been folded into the wet ingredients, since the bicarbonate's chemical action starts as soon as it comes in contact with moisture. However, there is no need to rush the pudding to the table when the cooking time is up—it behaves well if kept briefly over very low heat, or in a warm oven.

The sauce can be made any time you have five minutes to spare. Buy one of the better brands of apricot jam—I prefer a very tart one. This jam and the dried apricots produce a sharpness that counteracts the richness of the pudding and is surprisingly refreshing. I never add sugar to the sauce, but this is a matter of taste. Some of my friends and students serve whipped cream with it, a practice that I personally find unnecessary. However, I do have a personal vice where this dessert is concerned: if there is any left over I slice and fry it in butter, then sprinkle it with powdered cinnamon.

And a final word of advice: I assure that my guests and students accept a second helping by refraining from giving them too large helpings. I find it oppressive to be served a plate piled high with food, when it is an easy matter to have more should you want it and an effortless way to maintain a trim waistline if you don't.

Filet de Porc Sauvage (Marinated Shoulder Butt of Pork)

> 2 pork shoulder butts or cushions,
> approximately 2½ to 3 lbs. each, with
> all visible fat removed, tied as
> nearly as possible in sausage shape.

Marinade:

> 2 cups red wine (good Bordeaux or Burgundy)
> ⅓ cup chopped onion (1 small onion)
> 1 clove garlic, crushed
> 1 bay leaf
> 2 Tbsp. salt
> 4 or 5 twists of the black pepper mill
> ¼ cup finely chopped carrot
> ¼ cup finely chopped celery
> ¼ tsp. sage

> 1 Tbsp. oil, to be used for searing pork.

Mix all the marinade ingredients. Wipe both tied rolls of pork with paper towels and put them in a glass or enamel container just large enough to hold them. Souse with the marinade and turn them twice to make sure they are liberally coated. Turn them every half hour for 3 to 4 hours, or put the dish in the refrigerator overnight and turn them when you think of it, the oftener the better. Remove from the refrigerator 5 or 6 hours before cooking time.

Heat the oven to 350°F.

Wipe the pork dry after removing it from the marinade. Heat the 1 Tbsp. oil in a heavy skillet and brown the pork evenly on all sides. Put both pieces in an ovenproof dish just large enough to hold them with a tight-fitting lid and strain the marinade over them. Or to produce a thicker sauce, you may pour the marinade over the port unstrained and before serving it force the solids through a sieve or strainer. Cover, put in the oven and cook for 2 hours and serve with the sauce from the casserole.

Broccoli Harlequin

    1 small head cauliflower
    2 heads broccoli
    4 Tbsp. butter
    2 - 3 Tbsp. sour cream (optional)
    2 Tbsp. grated Parmesan cheese
    Salt and pepper
    ¾ cup bread crumbs tossed in
    3 Tbsp. melted butter

Heat the oven to 350°F.

Break the cauliflower into small heads and remove most of the white stalk. Prepare the broccoli by removing about half the coarse stems and breaking it into smaller heads. Cook the cauliflower 3 to 4 minutes in a good quantity of boiling salted water (1 Tbsp. salt to each quart of water) and, while still firm, lift out and drain. Cook the broccoli standing stalk down in the same water, covering the pot with a piece of cheesecloth. (The broken-up broccoli will take 5 to 6 minutes.) Drain the broccoli and purée it in a blender with the 4 Tbsp. butter and, if you wish, the 2 - 3 Tbsp. sour cream (this will assist in the blending).

Butter a 4 to 6 cup ovenproof dish, mound the cauliflower in it and sprinkle with the 2 Tbsp. grated Parmesan and 4 or 5 twists of the pepper mill. Season the broccoli purée with salt and pepper to taste, then spoon it over the cauliflower and sprinkle the top with the buttered bread crumbs. Put in the oven and bake for 20 minutes.

Endive Salad

    5 to 6 heads endive
    2 Tbsp. freshly chopped parsley

Vinaigrette Dressing:

> 2 Tbsp. red wine vinegar
> 6 Tbsp. olive oil
> 2 tsp. imported French mustard
> 2 tsp. lemon juice
> 1 tsp. salt
> pepper to taste

To prepare the dressing, combine all the ingredients in a screw-top jar and mix well.

Leaving the heads whole, wash and dry the endive. Be sure to remove any discolored outer leaves, then cut a wedge-shaped piece from the root end—this removes the hard core. Slice the endive thinly on the bias; you should have large, thin ovals. Mix the endive slices in a bowl with the vinaigrette dressing and the chopped parsley. This salad will not wilt and may be dressed half an hour before it is to be served. However, the parsley must be chopped only at the last minute, or it will lose its flavor.

The serving of the Fontina we discussed in the introductory notes—just remember to take it out of the refrigerator an hour or two before it's to go to the table.

Apricot Pudding with Apricot Sauce

> ¼ lb. (1 stick) unsalted butter
> ½ cup dark brown sugar, tightly packed
> 2 large eggs, lightly beaten
> 4 heaping Tbsp. apricot jam
> 6 dried apricots, finely diced
> ¼ cup chopped walnuts
> 1 cup all-purpose flour
> ½ tsp. bicarbonate of soda
> 1 Tbsp. butter and granulated sugar for the mold
> 1-quart pudding mold (or bowl)
> Pan with lid big enough to hold the mold or bowl

Apricot Sauce:

> ¾ cup apricot jam
> ½ cup water
> Juice of 1 lemon

Grease the inside of the mold with the 1 Tbsp. butter and dust it lightly with granulated sugar. Fill the pan with enough water to come halfway up the side of the mold or bowl and set it over low heat—you will want it to have come to a boil by the time you are ready to cook the pudding.

Beat the butter until it's soft and creamy with an electric hand beater or with a large wooden spoon. Add the brown sugar and continue beating until you have a light-brown-colored creamy mixture. Stir in the beaten eggs and apricot jam. The mixture will now look curdled, but this is as it should be. Stir in the finely diced apricots and the walnuts.

Sift together the flour and baking soda—if you don't have a flour sifter, use a wooden spoon to push the flour through a wire sieve. Fold the flour quickly into the egg mixture, and spoon into the prepared mold or bowl.

If you are using a bowl or a mold without a lid, cover it with waxed paper, then foil and tie it securely with string. Lower into the pan of boiling water, making sure the water reaches halfway up the mold or bowl. Reduce the heat until the water is simmering gently. Cover the pot with a lid and cook for at least one hour, but not more than an hour and a half. (Check the water level from time to time to make sure the pot hasn't boiled dry.)

To make the apricot sauce, stir apricot jam, water and lemon juice in a small saucepan over low heat, until thick. While still hot, force through fine sieve or strainer. It can now be set aside for reheating when the pudding has finished cooking.

To serve the pudding, run a knife around its edge and turn it out on a warm platter. Slice it in wedges like a cake, and pass the apricot sauce separately.

WINTER DINNER

Braised Jerusalem Artichokes
Saucisson en Brioche with Mushroom and Madeira Sauce
Haricots Verts
Apple and Grapefruit Compote

Serves 6 to 8

At first sight, this menu for a winter dinner party looks like a formidable amount of work. But if, as always, you will take the time in advance to read through all the instructions and organize your plan of attack (what may be done a day or two before, as well as the order in which you will set about working the day of the dinner itself), you will find it a very manageable enterprise.

The marketing may be completed a day or two before, except for the mushrooms and green beans. The fruit may in fact benefit from an extra day's ripening. The brown sauce which forms the base for the Mushroom and Madeira Sauce can be made as far in advance as you wish—I generally prepare a large quantity and freeze it (I can never see the point of messing up the kitchen to make a single serving of such a useful item).

The Jerusalem is not an artichoke, has nothing to do with Europe or the Middle East and is not even a distant cousin of the French globe artichoke. It belongs to the sunflower family and its natural home is America, from where it was introduced to Europe in the 17th century. It grows underground like a potato, and in fact looks rather like a potato covered with warts. It's the very devil to peel, but to me, at least, well worth the trouble, as I have loved this rather sweet and starchy vegetable since early childhood.

Choose firm tubers—if they are not as firm as you would like, leave them to soak in very cold water for several hours and they will perk up again. After peeling them, keep them in cold water to which you have added a little vinegar or lemon juice, which saves them from discoloring. To my mind, they are best served at room temperature, so you may want to cook them ahead to leave sufficient time for cooling.

The brioche dough will have to be made at least the day before in order to allow it at least eight hours' rest in the refrigerator. Once the dough has

27

been prepared, allowed to rise and punched down again, it may be set in a bowl in the refrigerator for as long as three or four days or can be frozen successfully.

The sausage you should use for this dish is coteghini, a spicy Italian sausage with a predominating—although not overpowering—aroma of garlic. It varies in size and shape—it may be short and thick or longer and thinner—but it is solid meat without a trace of filler, and may be purchased at most good Italian foodstores.

Be sure to choose mushrooms with caps that are tightly closed, with the underneath closely clamped to the stalk—this indicates youth and freshness. Mushrooms should not be washed under running water, but simply wiped with a damp cloth and their stalks cut off flush with the caps. The Madeira for the sauce should be the dry variety.

Buy small, crisp, bright green beans—not an easy task unless you live in the country. If it is impossible to find fresh beans, I suggest the following preliminary treatment of frozen ones: Thaw the beans at room temperature or under warm running water, then drop them into a quantity of boiling salted water. When the water returns to a boil, drain them immediately and toss them lightly in butter. This is all the cooking they need, since they'll later be reheated and tossed again in butter.

For the compote, try to get pink seedless grapefruit, which are on the market at this time of year. The best apple to use with the grapefruit is the Yellow Delicious, firm and juicy; otherwise, I'd recommend a good Macintosh. And if you are one of the fortunates who live where herbs grow in winter, a few fresh mint leaves add sparkle.

Braised Jerusalem Artichokes

    2 lbs. Jerusalem artichokes
    A little vinegar or lemon juice
    2 cups dry red wine
    4 Tbsp. butter
    1 tsp. salt
    Freshly ground black pepper
    2 Tbsp. finely chopped parsley

Heat the over to 350°F.

Peel the artichokes—a good, sharp paring knife is essential—and put them in a bowl of water with a little vinegar or lemon juice until they're all ready for the oven, then drain them. Put the artichokes, red wine, butter, salt and pepper in a heavy pan with a tight-fitting lid. Bring to a boil on top of the stove, then cover and cook in the oven for 30 minutes. Test for doneness with a fork or toothpick—they should be firm but admit the fork, rather like properly done potatoes.

Take the artichokes out of the liquid with a slotted spoon. Reduce the liquid in the pan to ¾ cup over high heat, and pour it over the artichokes. Serve them at room temperature, sprinkled liberally with chopped parsley.

Saucisson en Brioche

    2 large Italian coteghini, 1½ to 2 lbs. each
    1 recipe brioche dough
    Glaze: 1 egg yolk beaten with 2 Tbsp. cream

Brioche Dough:

    2 packages dry yeast
    ¼ cup warm milk
    2 tsp. sugar
    3 cups all-purpose flour
    1 tsp. salt
    4 eggs
    ½ lb. (2 sticks) softened butter

To make the dough, sprinkle both packages of dry yeast over the warm milk. Add the 2 tsp. sugar, stir once and set aside. Sift the flour and salt together into a large bowl (or into the bowl of an electric mixer, if you have one with a dough hook). Make a well in the flour and break in the 4 eggs. Add the softened yeast and stir until smooth. I begin mixing with a large wooden spoon, and later on use my right hand to work it, leaving the left one clean for picking up things. Or use the dough hook with a medium speed on an electric mixer.

Add the softened butter. It should look and feel like cream—don't let it soften beyond this point or you will have an oily mass. Work the butter into the dough until it has been completely absorbed. If you are using your hand, slap the dough around till it takes on an elastic quality and is inclined to leave the side of the bowl. (This will happen much faster in the mixer, but the final result will be the same.) It is now ready for its resting and rising period. Turn it into a clean bowl, dusted lightly with flour. Shape it into a ball and slash it deeply in the shape of a cross with a sharp knife (it will rise more easily than if left in a single heavy mass). Cover the bowl with a clean towel and leave it in a snug, draft-free corner of the kitchen to rise. In about 1 to 1½ hours it should have doubled in size. Punch it down with the back of your hand to deflate it. Cover the bowl with plastic wrap and put it in the refrigerator for a minimum of eight hours, or most conveniently, overnight.

Two or 3 hours before dinner, preheat the oven to 375°F.

Cover the sausages with cold water in a pan large enough to hold them comfortably and bring to a boil. Cover, lower the heat and simmer gently for 35 minutes. Drain and when cool enough to handle, remove the skins. Set aside—but do not refrigerate.

For the glaze, mix the yolk of 1 egg with 2 Tbsp. cream and have a brush ready.

Take the brioche dough from the refrigerator and roll it out on a floured board to a thickness of ¼-inch. Measure the sausages against the dough, making sure it's rolled out wide enough so that when wrapped around the sausage its ends will overlap. Cut to size. Draw both sides of the dough up and over the sausage, but before pressing them together brush both edges lightly with the egg yolk and cream glaze, which will seal the dough. Trim the ends, leaving enough to fold and seal them envelope-shape. Again, brush with the glaze before sealing.

Put the wrapped sausages on a baking sheet, seam side down. There is no need to butter the sheet, as there is ample butter in the brioche. Make sure the seams are neatly pinched. Roll out the remaining dough and make cut-outs with which to decorate the surface of the brioche. Then brush the surface of the brioche with the glaze before pressing them into place. (I have a liking for strips of dough laid lattice-fashion over the surface, rather like the lacing on a gladiator's leg.)

If you are not going to bake it right away, put the baking sheet in the refrigerator. When you're ready to bake it, brush the entire surface with the glaze again and slide it onto the middle shelf of the oven for 30 to 35 minutes. After the first 15 minutes, brush again with the glaze, which will produce a wonderful golden-brown finish. After taking it out of the oven, let it stand for 10 or 15 minutes, as it is then easier to carve. I'd suggest using a serrated knife to make slices ½ to ¾ inches thick, and serving with a spatula.

Mushroom and Madeira Sauce

    ¼ lb. fresh mushrooms
    3 cups brown sauce
    ¾ cup dry Madeira
    Salt and pepper

Brown Sauce:

    6 Tbsp. butter, oil or bacon fat
    ⅓ cup finely chopped carrots
    ⅓ cup finely chopped onion
    ⅓ cup finely chopped celery
    ½ cup finely chopped lean ham (about 2 oz.)
    4 Tbsp. flour
    6 cups beef stock, canned beef bouillon
      or bouillon prepared from cubes
    2 Tbsp. tomato paste
    1 bay leaf

    1 small bunch parsley
    8 peppercorns
    2 or 3 chopped mushrooms (optional)

For the brown sauce, melt the butter, oil or bacon fat in a heavy 2- or 3-quart pot with a lid. Add the vegetables and ham, cover and cook over low heat for 15 minutes. (By using the lid you will eliminate the necessity to stir—condensation will drip back into the pan to prevent scorching.) Then stir in the flour and cook slowly, stirring, until the mixture turns brown. Don't worry if it appears to scorch slightly—you want it to turn brown. Ten minutes should be sufficient.

Off heat pour in the beef stock and blend with a wire whisk. Stir in the tomato paste and add the bay leaf, parsley, peppercorns and optional mushrooms. Bring to a boil and reduce the heat so that it boils steadily but not fiercely. Reduce the liquid by one-quarter—i.e., boil it until one-quarter has evaporated. Strain and set aside.

Wipe the ¼ lb. mushrooms with a clean damp cloth. Cut off their stalks flush with the caps. Slice very thin—if they are large, cut them in half before slicing.

In a heavy pan, combine the 3 cups of brown sauce and the mushrooms. Cook over medium heat for 5 minutes. Add the Madeira and simmer 4 or 5 minutes longer. Correct the seasoning, if needed, by adding more salt and freshly ground black pepper.

Serve in a well-warmed sauceboat.

Haricots Verts

    3 lbs. fresh green beans
    2 Tbsp. salt
    3 Tbsp. butter
    Salt and freshly ground black pepper

Bring 2 quarts of fresh water to a rolling boil in a 3-quart, heavy-bottomed pan. Cut off the tops and tails of the beans with a pair of scissors, dropping them as they are trimmed into a bowl of very cold water. When the beans are ready, add the 2 Tbsp. salt to the boiling water, then toss in the beans by the handful, attempting to keep the water at the boil. Cook for 4 minutes after the last of the beans have been added and the water has again come to a boil. They should now be done al dente—crisp and still green—but test one with your teeth, the only way to make sure. Plunge the beans into a large bowl of cold water (or into a sinkful of cold water) to stop their cooking any further, then drain and set them aside. This may be done in the morning of the day they are to be eaten, if you like.

Five or 10 minutes before serving them, melt the 3 Tbsp. butter in the heavy pan and toss the beans over medium heat until they are hot. Season with salt and pepper.

Apple and Grapefruit Compote

    3 pink seedless grapefruit
    6 apples, preferably Yellow Delicious
    Sugar syrup, if needed
    3-4 sprigs fresh mint

Sugar Syrup:

    ¼ cup water
    ½ cup sugar

Peel the grapefruit with a sharp knife over a large bowl, removing all the white pith and allowing the juice to drip into the bowl. Cut the sections free of the surrounding membranes, dropping them into the bowl. When all the sections have been cut out, squeeze the membranes to get the last drops of their juice. Peel and core the apples. Slice them into thin wedges, adding them to the grapefruit sections immediately. The citrus juice will prevent discoloration.

If the grapefruit haven't produced enough juice to cover the fruit to your satisfaction, prepare the syrup: Dissolve the sugar in the ¼ cup water and simmer gently for 3 or 4 minutes. Set aside to cool, then add as much as needed to the fruit in the bowl. Chill until needed. Remove from the refrigerator at least an hour before serving and garnish with sprigs of mint.

SUNDAY BRUNCH

Scrambled Eggs and Smoked Salmon
Casserole of Spinach
Toasted Whole Wheat Pita
Marmalade   Black Currant Jam
Almond Tart

Serves 6 to 8

Brunch is something I've never quite understood, for to create another meal for a day that already has three seems to me rather unnecessary. However, I have been quite firmly instructed by my students that many of them are in the habit of making a single midday meal do the work of breakfast and lunch. On the strength of this I go along with brunch and look upon myself as an oddity from another age who celebrates each new day with a square meal.

I am particularly fond of this menu which, to my way of thinking, might still be called breakfast. I would first offer Bloody Mary's to my guests. I can see absolutely no reason why one shouldn't have a Bloody Mary at 10 A.M. It can't do any more harm than it would two or three hours later in the day, and whether this is considered a suitable hour for a drink is simply a matter of habit and convention. A hundred years ago or later there was nothing out of the ordinary about a breakfast of steak, cheese and beer or in the 18th century, a bottle of claret. Scrambled eggs are convention itself, and smoked salmon is one of the most delightful additions to eggs I can think of. Spinach is unexpected at this time of day, but creamed and cooked in a casserole it goes very well indeed with the eggs. As for the almond tart, I don't think anyone will hesitate to serve something sweet at whatever hour of the day.

Scrambled eggs for me must be moist and creamy and made without cream or milk, but only butter. It's rather a tricky business to get them right for a large number of people, but I have acquired a very useful practice from the cook of some English friends. It is to scramble all the eggs with the exception of two or three, depending upon the number needed altogether, keeping them warm as they are finished. If the mixture begins to look overdry, you can mix in briefly the two or three eggs set aside. For this meal, they can then be kept warm briefly on a hot plate

37

after the chopped smoked salmon is stirred in—the smoked salmon helps keep them moist.

The spinach may be prepared and puréed well ahead of time, and the casserole put together early in the morning or the evening before. It can then be heated in the oven for about half an hour while you are preparing the scrambled eggs.

Pita is the unleavened bread found throughout the Middle East. It is now available in many supermarkets as well as in specialty stores, often labeled as Armenian bread. Buy the whole wheat variety, which I find particularly delicious, if you can find it and overestimate the quantity you will need, as you'll find that it disappears with astonishing speed. I split it carefully in half horizontally, then cut each half in four, buttering and toasting it, then reheating it in the oven before serving. In addition to the marmalade, I've suggested offering black currant jam—buy a good imported brand from the British Isles or Canada, since black currants aren't grown in this country.

The almond tart should not be refrigerated. It may safely be made the night before, or you might want to mix and then refrigerate the dough overnight, rolling it out and finishing the tart in the morning. This is a particularly rich and flaky dough which is extremely good with the almond filling.

Scrambled Eggs and Smoked Salmon

2 large eggs per person, plus 3 extra for every 10 eggs

For every 2 eggs:
1 Tbsp. unsalted butter
½ slice smoked salmon, chopped
1 tsp. finely chopped parsley

Freshly ground black pepper
Sprigs of parsley (optional)

We will start with 10 eggs (any more become difficult to manage) and about 3 slices of chopped smoked salmon. Melt 5 Tbsp. butter in the top part of a double boiler directly over low heat and mix the eggs in a bowl (but do not beat them to a froth). Add the eggs to the pan with the melted butter and stand it over boiling water, stirring to mix. Continue stirring until curds are formed. If the mixture appears to be cooking too quickly take the pan off the boiling water and continue to stir. Mix in the chopped smoked salmon and cook until the mixture is creamy and curd-like.

If the eggs now have to wait while you do more for additional guests, set them aside and, just before they are to be served, put the pan over low heat and stir in the 3 extra eggs. The addition of the 3 uncooked eggs will keep the mixture soft and moist while they are being heated. Finally, season with freshly ground black pepper (it is unlikely that salt will be needed) and stir in the chopped parsley. Serve on a heated platter garnished, if you wish, with sprigs of parsley. If you are the owner of 2 double boilers the second mixture could be prepared at the same time, but over lower heat so that it will cook slowly.

Casserole of Spinach

6 10-oz. packets frozen chopped spinach
6 Tbsp. butter
1 cup finely chopped onion
2 cups sour cream

Freshly grated nutmeg
Salt and freshly ground black pepper
½ cup bread crumbs
2 Tbsp. grated Parmesan cheese
Ovenproof dish holding approximately 2 quarts
    or a 2-quart soufflé dish, buttered

Heat the oven to 350°F.

Defrost the spinach and drain it thoroughly. Melt 4 Tbsp. of the butter in a skillet, add the chopped onion and sauté gently, being careful not to allow the onion to brown—it should be transparent.

Purée the spinach with the assistance of a little of the sour cream in a blender if you have one, otherwise force it through a strainer or sieve. Add the onion and the butter in which it has been sautéed, using more of the sour cream as it is needed. Then scrape the puréed spinach into a bowl and sir in any remaining sour cream. Season with grated nutmeg, salt and pepper—go lightly on the salt but make the nutmeg pronounced.

Melt the remaining 2 Tbsp. butter in the skillet and stir in the bread crumbs, coating them thoroughly with the butter. Spoon the spinach mixture into the buttered dish and sprinkle the top with the buttered bread crumbs and then with the grated Parmesan cheese. Cook in the 350° oven for 30 minutes or until hot.

For preparation of the pita, see the introductory notes.

Almond Tart

Pastry:

2 cups less 2 Tbsp. (8 oz.) flour
Pinch of salt
10 Tbsp. butter
4 - 8 Tbsp. ice water
2 Tbsp. lemon juice
1 egg yolk

Filling:

    4 oz. unsalted butter, softened
    4 oz. sugar
    4 Tbsp. heavy cream, whipped
    3 egg yolks
    ½ lb. ground almonds
    1 tsp. grated lemon rind

Glaze: 1 egg beaten with 2 Tbsp. milk
Granulated sugar

To make the pastry, sift together the flour and salt. Chip 2 Tbsp. of the butter into the flour and blend well with the fingertips. Make a well in the center and add 4 Tbsp. of the ice water, the lemon juice and the egg yolk, working the mixture to make a pliable paste. Add more ice water if necessary—4 more Tbsp. at most. Gather the pastry into a ball and roll it out into a rectangle about one-eighth inch thick.

Cut 4 Tbsp. of the butter into thin slices and spread it evenly over the rectangle of dough, taking care not to get it too close to the edge. Fold the pastry over in thirds, enclosing the butter. Roll out again to another rectangle and spread another 4 Tbsp. butter as before. Fold and roll the dough 3 additional times, making 5 in all. (Mark the dough with a finger to keep track.) Fold in thirds for the final time and place the dough in the refrigerator to rest for one hour.

Heat the oven to 425° F.

To make the filling, cream together until smooth the 4 oz. softened butter and the 4 oz. sugar. Whip the 4 Tbsp. heavy cream and beat the egg yolks into it lightly, then mix them gently into the butter and sugar. Stir in the ground almonds and the grated lemon rind and set aside while you roll out the pastry.

Remove the pastry from the refrigerator and divide it into 2 portions, one slightly larger than the other. Form the smaller into a ball and roll it out into a round about the thickness of 2 pennies. Transfer to a large greased baking sheet. Spread the filling mixture evenly over the pastry round, leaving a margin of about 1 inch around the edge.

Form the second (larger) pastry half into a ball and roll it out into a round slightly larger and thicker than the first. Dampen the edges of the bottom layer slightly with water, then lay the second round over it and press the edges together lightly. Trim the edge and notch all around. Make a lattice on the top, cutting the pastry not quite all the way through. Glaze the top with the 1 egg beaten lightly with 2 Tbsp. milk and put the tart in the oven, immediately turning the heat down to 400°F. Remove from the oven after 35 minutes and brush with the glaze again, returning it to the oven for 10 minutes more. If it appears to be becoming too brown, cover with a piece of foil or greaseproof paper. Remove the tart from the oven and sprinkle it with granulated sugar.

Serve either warm or hot.

WINTER BUFFET

Hot Cheese Profiteroles
Marinated Mushrooms
Turkey with Chestnuts   *Scallops in White Wine*
Salad   *Green Rice*
Frozen Chocolate Mousse   *Pineapple with Kirsch*

Serves 18 to 20

The buffet service has many advantages. It is the only way to have more than four for a meal if you have a small kitchen and no dining room. And even if you can seat a modest number of people, it's the only sensible way to entertain more than eight or ten for dinner if you do it without help. It can be an economical although lavish meal, with the single exception in this menu of the cost of the scallops, and doesn't require your spending the day in the kitchen—practically all of the preparation and cooking can be done beforehand, leaving only the reheating and final assembling of the dishes for the evening of the party itself.

Although a buffet is an informal meal, don't make the mistake of neglecting a single detail in its planning. Keep in mind your store of pots and pans, and don't forget to take into account the capacity of your stove. Unless you wish to rent or borrow glass and china and tableware, don't ask more guests than you have equipment. Do as I do and make out a work sheet four or five days before the party, starting with a shopping list—you may come across some of the ingredients you'll need in advance of shopping specifically for the meal. A work sheet is equally useful to chart your progress in preparing the various dishes during the several days before the party, and in helping you organize efficiently and without fear of forgetting anything the last-minute details. A final note: I make it a principle to serve bite-size pieces of everything so that knives are unnecessary.

Do by all means avoid the error of putting out all the food at once, with the result that the buffet table looks like a picked-over bargain counter after the first five minutes. Choose serving dishes that are small rather than too large, and reserve half the food in the kitchen. After the first onslaught, you can then replenish the serving casseroles and platters. If the dishes have been thoroughly heated, they should stay hot until you get them back to the kitchen to refill them—and it is rarely necessary to do this more than once. Even the chocolate mousse may be cut in half after it has been frozen, and brought to the table as needed.

Now that we've had the order of battle, here are some details: Make, fill and freeze the profiteroles (small puffs made from the standard cream puff or choux paste) as far ahead of time as you wish, taking them out of the freezer an hour before your guests arrive. They should be heated in small batches on a baking sheet in a 325° oven, after trying a single one to see how long it takes. If you have only one oven, the baking sheet will fit on top of your casseroles if there is no room for it on a second shelf. I pass them not more than three or four times before the rest of the meal is put out.

The mushrooms should be wiped off with a damp cloth, then quartered if they are large—leave small ones whole. Cut off the stalks flush with the caps, and store them in a plastic bag in the refrigerator. Make the vinaigrette dressing in a screw-top jar in the morning (including enough to use for the salad), but don't refrigerate it. A little over an hour before serving time, toss the mushrooms in the dressing, let them stand for an hour, then drain and sprinkle them liberally with freshly chopped parsley. (The dressing should be set aside again until time to use it on the salad—it will be distinctly improved by its encounter with the mushrooms.) Pile the mushrooms on a platter around a shot glass full of plain wooden cocktail sticks, and let your guests help themselves.

Both the turkey and scallop casseroles may be made in advance and frozen if necessary, although I don't advise this. If you have the time, cook them a day or so ahead and simply consign them to the refrigerator. Be sure to cool them uncovered, unless you protect them with foil and several layers of paper or cloth from the condensation which will form under their lids. And as always, allow them to cool before refrigerating and refrigerate first if you are going to freeze them. Reverse the process to reheat and serve; allow them first to reach room temperature, then heat them gently.

The rice may be cooked al dente in the late afternoon—either according to package directions, if you use a packaged rice, or by my uncomplicated method of cooking in plenty of boiling salted water until it suits my taste. Then put it in a pan and cover with a clean kitchen towel. If you have room, put it in the oven half an hour before eating time to reheat. The parsley should be chopped and stirred into the rice just before serving.

Unless you can rely on your fruit man to provide you with two fully ripened pineapples on request, you should shop for them well in advance. Consult him in any case to choose pineapples that will be ripe on the appointed day—a ripe pineapple is a luscious fruit, vastly different from the painfully difficult to chew and not yet flavorful fruit one is usually served. Also, the female fruit, if you can get it, is sweeter than the male and may be distinguished by finding among its leaves tight clusters of much smaller leaves.

The frozen mousse may be made as much as a week beforehand. Take it out of the freezer and unmold it about half an hour before it is to be eaten, and put it in the refrigerator to soften a bit. The mousse and the pineapples should be brought together to the table after everything else has been cleared away.

Hot Cheese Profiteroles

Choux Paste:

>   1 cup water
>   6 Tbsp. unsalted butter
>   1 cup, less 1 Tbsp. sifted flour
>   3 large eggs
>   Glaze: 1 egg beaten with 1 Tbsp. water

Cheese Filling:

>   6 Tbsp. unsalted butter
>   6 Tbsp. flour
>   2 cups milk, heated almost to a boil
>   2 tsp. salt
>   2 tsp. pepper
>   8 Tbsp. Parmesan cheese, grated
>   1 Tbsp. prepared mustard
>   1 tsp. Worcestershire sauce

Heat the oven to 400° F.

To make the choux paste, combine the water and butter in a heavy saucepan. Cook over low heat until the butter has melted, then raise the heat and bring to a boil. Add the flour all at once, remove from the heat and beat vigorously with a wooden spoon until the paste comes away from the sides of the pan. Transfer the paste to a large mixing bowl and allow to cool, then add one egg at a time, beating after each until it is completely absorbed. (If you have an electric mixer, use its dough-mixing arm; it takes the work out of this operation.) Fit a pastry bag with a plain tube, fill it half full and squeeze out mounds of paste no larger than a heaping teaspoonful onto a lightly greased baking sheet. Or shape large teaspoonful of the paste directly on the baking sheet with a spoon. Place them far enough apart to allow for their doubling in size and repeat until the past is used up. To make the glaze, heat 1 egg with 1 Tbsp. water, then brush each puff with it. Reduce the oven temperature to 350° and bake for 30 minutes, or until puffed and golden brown. Remove from the oven to cool.

For the filling, melt the butter in a saucepan, stir in the flour and cook over medium heat for 3 minutes, stirring this roux (the term for this primary combination of flour and butter) constantly. Don't allow it to color. Off heat, add the hot milk all at once, beating with a wire whisk to make a smooth paste. Add the salt, pepper and cheese, stirring until the cheese is melted, then add the mustard and Worcestershire sauce. Return to the heat and cook 2 minutes longer, stirring, then allow the mixture to cool.

Fill a pastry bag fitted with a small tube half full of the cheese filling. Pierce the underside of each profiterole and force in the cheese mixture to fill. (Or do this by hand using a small spoon, being careful not to tear too large a hole in the profiteroles.) The filled profiteroles may now be refrigerated or frozen. To serve, reheat in a 325° oven for about 25 minutes or until thoroughly hot (try one first to get the exact timing).

Marinated Mushrooms

    1 lb. fresh mushrooms, preferably no bigger
       than one inch in diameter
       (halve or quarter them if they are larger)
    Vinaigrette dressing (see page 23); 1 mixing
       for the mushrooms, or 2 to have ample for
       the salad as well
    2 Tbsp. finely chopped parsley

Wipe the mushrooms clean with a damp cloth. Cut off the stems flush with the caps, discarding them unless you use them for some other purpose. Mix with the dressing and set aside for an hour. Drain, reserving the dressing for the salad. Just before serving, sprinkle the mushrooms with the parsley and heap them on a platter around a shot glass full of wooden cocktail sticks.

Turkey with Chestnuts

    1 oz. dried mushrooms
    1 cup boiling water
    8 Tbsp. butter

5 lbs. raw turkey breast (or the frozen "turkey
   roast" sold in supermarkets), cut in 1-inch cubes
6 Tbsp. brandy
2 Tbsp. finely chopped onion
4 cloves of garlic, chopped
2 tsp. meat glaze (Bovril)
2 Tbsp. tomato paste
6 Tbsp. flour
2 cups chicken or turkey stock
1 cup dry white Bordeaux wine
Salt and freshly ground black pepper
½ lb. cooked chestnuts, cut in ¼-inch dice
   (slit the chestnuts in the shape of a cross,
     roast them for 30 minutes in a 375° oven,
     then peel and dice)
1½ cups sour cream
½ cup finely chopped parsley

One hour before preparing, cover the dried mushrooms with 1 cup boiling water and set aside.

Heat the oven to 350°F.

Cut the turkey or turkey roast into 1-inch cubes. Melt the butter in a skillet and brown the turkey cubes, a few at a time. Add a little more butter during the browning, if necessary. Transfer the cubes as they are done to an ovenproof casserole with a lid. After all the turkey has been browned and placed in the casserole, put the skillet back over low heat and add the brandy to whatever juices there are in the skillet, scraping to loosen the bits which have stuck to the side during the process of browning.

Drain the mushrooms, reserving the liquid. Chop them finely, and add them with the onion and garlic to the liquid in the skillet. Stir in the meat glaze, tomato paste and flour, mixing thoroughly over low heat. Gradually add the mushroom liquid, chicken or turkey stock and white wine. Cook the mixture slowly, stirring constantly, until the sauce thickens. Season to taste with salt and pepper, then pour the sauce over the turkey in the casserole and mix in the cooked chestnuts. Cover and bake 35 minutes or until tender. Stir in the sour cream and reheat very briefly. After the sour cream has been added, don't allow it to come to a boil again, as it would then curdle. Sprinkle with the chopped parsley just before serving. If the casserole is to be frozen or refrigerated, do not stir in the sour cream until it has been defrosted and/or reheated.

Scallops in White Wine

     ½ lb. (2 sticks) butter
    10 shallots, finely chopped
     6 lbs. bay scallops
     4 cups dry white Bordeaux wine
     3 Tbsp. salt
     1 lb. mushrooms, trimmed and quartered
    1½ tsp. pepper
     2 cups heavy cream
    Bottled clam juice or more heavy cream
     8 Tbsp. rice flour (may be purchased in
        Chinese or Japanese stores)
     1 cup finely chopped parsley

Melt 8 Tbsp. of the butter in a heavy, 4- to 6-quart enamel or stainless steel pot, stir in the shallots and cook gently, stirring constantly, until they are transparent. Add the scallops and cook, stirring frequently, until the scallops are tender. Remove the scallops from the liquid and set them aside in a casserole while you finish the sauce.

Cook the mushrooms in the liquid from which you've taken the scallops for 2 to 3 minutes—no longer. Stir in the pepper and heavy cream. Lift the mushrooms out with a slotted spoon and add them to the scallops in the casserole. To prepare the sauce, measure out the scallop liquid and add enough heavy cream or bottled clam juice to make up 8 cups. Work the rice flour and the remaining 8 Tbsp. butter together with a wooden spoon until smooth, then add bit by bit to the sauce and cook over low heat, stirring constantly, until it thickens (about 12 to 15 minutes). Taste for seasoning—a further 2 Tbsp. salt may be needed. Pour the sauce over the scallops and mushrooms, and sprinkle with the finely chopped parsley.

The dish may now be cooled, covered and refrigerated, taking care not to let condensed moisture drip into and thin the sauce. It should be reheated in a 325° oven for 30 minutes or until heated through.

Salad

> ½ head of escarole
> 2 heads of Boston lettuce
> 1 small iceberg lettuce
> 1 small bunch parsley
> ¼ lb. Gruyère cheese, diced
> Vinaigrette dressing (already prepared
>   for the Marinated Mushrooms)

Wash and dry the parsley and the salad greens except for the iceberg lettuce, and refrigerate, if you like. When you're ready to assemble the salad, wash and dry the iceberg lettuce, then tear it, all the Boston lettuce and the half head of escarole into small bite-sized pieces. Remove the parsley sprigs from the stalks and chop half of them very fine, leaving the rest whole. Mix all the greens with the parsley sprigs, the chopped parsley and the diced cheese. Set aside one-half of this salad, and toss the other with half of the vinaigrette dressing. Reserve the balance of each to replenish the salad bowl later on.

Green Rice

> 4 cups your favorite long-grain rice
> 3 quarts fiercely boiling water
> 3 Tbsp. salt
> Freshly ground black pepper
> 1 tightly packed cup parsley sprigs, finely chopped

Cook the rice according to package directions, or pour it into the boiling water to which you've added the salt, stirring the while. When it comes to a boil again, reduce the heat until the water boils gently, scrape the bottom of the pan to make sure none of the uncooked rice has stuck to it, and cook for about 12 minutes, uncovered. When the 12 minutes are up, test a grain between your teeth—it should be firm, but not brittle on the inside. If it is brittle, cook for 2 or 3 minutes longer, or until it tastes right to you.

Drain the rice into a wire strainer or colander and run cold water over it to stop its cooking. Set it aside in a large roasting pan covered with a clean towel, and when ready to reheat, put it in a 325° oven for about half an hour. Correct the seasoning by adding salt and pepper to your taste and stir in the chopped parsley at the last minute.

Frozen Chocolate Mousse

> 2 packages (or about 30) ladyfingers—commercial
>   will do, although those from a bakery are better
>   and French champagne are best
> 1 Tbsp. butter
> Loaf tin 2½ x 4½ x 11½ inches or a 2-quart mold
> Waxed paper
>
> 10 oz. Baker's unsweetened chocolate
> 5 oz. Baker's semi-sweet chocolate
> 1 cup sugar
> ⅓ cup hot water
> 3 egg whites
> ¼ tsp. cream of tartar
> Pinch of salt
> 1 tsp. vanilla extract
> 2 cups heavy cream, very cold
> ⅓ cup rum, chocolate liqueur or
>   Grand Marnier or other orange liqueur

Line the loaf tin or mold with waxed paper, cutting the bottom to fit and the sides so that they stand about 1 inch above the edge. Before putting the waxed paper in place, dab a very small amount of butter on the side that will go next to the tin—this will hold it in place and will enable you to unmold the mousse easily. Fit the ladyfingers around the sides of the tin or mold, using a small dab of butter on each to hold them upright. (If French champagne biscuits are used, alternate their thick and thin ends.) Cover the bottom with the ladyfingers, filling in the spaces with crushed ones.

Chop up the chocolate and melt it over warm water. In a separate pan, dissolve the sugar in the ⅓ cup hot water and set it over a low flame. In an electric mixer, or with a hand beater, beat the egg whites until they are white and foamy. Add the cream of tartar and pinch of salt, then beat until they hold definite peaks and mix in the vanilla extract. Meanwhile, raise the heat under the sugar syrup and boil until it reaches 238° on a candy thermometer or the soft ball stage. Pour it over the egg whites in a thin, steady stream while beating and continue to beat until they are cool, firm and shiny.

Pour the chilled heavy cream into a bowl and put it in the freezer for about 10 minutes. Meanwhile, stir the melted chocolate until smooth and glossy and when it's cool, stir it into the egg whites with a large metal spoon just long enough to mix thoroughly. Take the bowl of chilled cream from the freezer, add the rum or liqueur and beat with a rotary beater until a distinct ribbon forms on its surface. Fold this into the chocolate mixture, again just long enough to mix them thoroughly, and spoon the finished mousse into the prepared tin or mold. When it's full, let it drop from a few inches above the counter to settle it and fill up air pockets.

Freeze for at least 8 hours. If it is to be frozen for longer, seal it securely with plastic wrap. To unmold, run a metal spatula between the waxed paper and the tin or mold, put the serving platter over it, then reverse onto the platter—a tug or two on the waxed paper will release the mousse. Let it stand in the refrigerator for 20 minutes before serving and, if you like, put out only half on the buffet table at one time.

Pineapple with Kirsch

    2 ripe pineapples
    ½ cup Kirsch

Peel and core both pineapples and cut each into 8 slices. Pour the kirsch over the pineapple slices, being careful to spoon it over all the fruit, and refrigerate for at least an hour. Serve cold, with a dish of fine sugar available for those who may want it.

⚛ SPRING ⚛

Spring is officially recognized on March 21, when "again the golden day resum'd and ruled in just equation with the night." At the tender age of about six, when I took the seasons and their bounty for granted, spring for me was March 17, St. Patrick's Day, a holiday from school and classes. Disregarding sleet or snow, this was the day my friends and I bade good-by to winter and welcomed spring with a token plunge in the icy mountain river. Looking back on this ritual, it strikes me now as lunacy. But it never harmed us, and curiously enough, our parents or whoever was in charge never cautioned us against catching pneumonia, but warned us repeatedly of the risk of drowning.

A little later in life, spring was an endless flock of lambs in my mind's eye. One of the flock, the lamb that had been born before Christmas, ended its short life on the family table toward the middle of the month of April. At this tender age the bone was well set, yet not too much green food had been eaten to darken the flesh. And, of most importance, there had been no lack of moisture in the lamb's diet, the absence of which causes the strong aroma noticeable in lamb reared in dry climates.

Sorrel, young and tart, was picked in its native surroundings and used to make an unforgettable soup, fascinatingly rich and sharp. Rhubarb, grown under large up-ended earthenware pots, now had long tender pink stalks, the poisonous leaves a very pale, almost celadon green. The pink stalks went into a deep pie dish covered with a light, rich and short crust, baked golden and served with unwhipped cream from Jersey cows—cream that bears little resemblance to today's poor relative. Asparagus was plentiful, the thin green spears served with drawn butter as a separate course. We ate it then, as I do now, with fingers, never with a knife and fork.

There seemed no end to what the earth produced and each offering was enjoyed until a successor appeared to claim the scene. The cycle would be repeated until modern invention launched the frozen product—a great convenience certainly, affording us with strawberries in northern climes in December. But, although I admit to taking advantage of this progress, I infinitely prefer the local asparagus or strawberry in its own season.

SPRING LUNCHEON

Asparagus Vinaigrette
Crêpes de Volaille   Sauce Mornay
Strawberries Escoffier

Serves 6 to 8

Shop for the asparagus and strawberries in the morning or, at the very earliest, the afternoon before you serve this meal. Choose asparagus with tightly closed heads, crisp stalks and moist cut ends. This is a tall order, but if you find the asparagus with all the fine points except freshly cut ends, don't worry too much. When you get them home, cut off a little of the stalk and stand the bunch in cold water to freshen up. I prefer the medium asparagus to the very thick, and I like the color to be green rather than the pale blanched type so much appreciated in France—I think it has better flavor. And be sure not to overcook it, a misuse of this vegetable that I find repellent.

Choose a three-and-a-half- to four-pound chicken. Cook it very slowly, and keep the stock to be used as the prime ingredient for a superb soup. Stock freezes well, and has so many uses that it's well worth while to freeze it in usefully sized containers. I use one-cup measures for the later preparation of sauces, and quart measures as the basis for soups. When the stock is frozen solid, it can be released from its container by dipping it briefly in hot water; then wrap the frozen block in plastic wrap and in foil and return it to the freezer. In this way your containers are not put out of commission for the life of the frozen stock and the frozen bricks stack neatly. Any chicken not used in the crêpes will make a salad for another meal or may be used to fill sandwiches.

The crêpes may be made at any time and refrigerated or frozen. Whenever you do it, make a quantity for another day as well: I usually do two or three batches at once, since there is little in the way of filling that can't be wrapped in a crêpe. They freeze beautifully if they are properly packed with a piece of waxed paper between each one, all securely wrapped and sealed in a plastic bag or box.

Choose firm, shiny strawberries. Wash them under cold running water, dry them on paper towels and then pull out the hull—if you hull them before washing, the water will seep in and leave them soggy. Toss them in the Escoffier dressing about an hour before serving. Don't refrigerate them, as this will deaden the flavor and the wonderful aroma.

Asparagus Vinaigrette

    3 lbs. medium asparagus
    2 mixings vinaigrette dressing (page 23)

With a sharp knife cut the asparagus in equal lengths, no longer than the width of the plate on which they are to be served. Scrape and remove the close-fitting scales toward the top with a vegetable peeler—they harbor sand and grit. Steep in cold water until they are to be cooked.

If you have an asparagus cooker, fill it with the required amount of water and bring to a boil. Stand the asparagus in the liner and cook uncovered for 4 to 5 minutes—cooked in this way, the tops will be crisp and the stalks tender. If you don't own an asparagus cooker, use a saucepan large enough to hold the asparagus. Add 1 Tbsp. of salt for each quart of water and, when the water has come to a boil, put in the asparagus, cooking for 4 to 5 minutes after the water has returned to a boil. Test a stalk—it should be firm, but not crunchy—then drain thoroughly and let the asparagus cool to room temperature.

I prefer serving the vinaigrette dressing in separate small dishes so that the asparagus can be dipped one at a time. This is less messy than pouring the sauce into the plate.

Crêpes de Volaille, Sauce Mornay

    3½- to 4-lb. chicken
    1 stalk celery with leaves
    1 carrot, scraped
    1 onion, peeled
    3 sprigs parsley
    1 bay leaf
    4 peppercorns
    1 tsp. salt

Crêpes:

> 1½ cups flour
> ½ tsp. salt
> ½ cup milk (approximately)
> 2 Tbsp. oil
> 2 eggs
> 2 egg yolks
> 2 cups milk (approximately)
> Oil for cooking

Sauce Mornay:

> 1 Tbsp. butter
> 4 Tbsp. flour
> 3 cups milk
> Salt and freshly ground pepper
> Nutmeg, freshly grated
> ¾ cup Parmesan cheese, freshly grated

To make the crêpes, combine the flour, salt and the ½ cup milk in a bowl. Add the 2 Tbsp. oil while stirring and continue stirring while adding the eggs and the egg yolks. Stir until the batter is smooth and thoroughly blended. Allow the batter to rest for at least 2 hours, then stir in the additional milk until the batter is the consistency of heavy cream.

Heat 1 Tbsp. of oil in a 6-inch crêpe pan. Pour off any excess oil and drop 2 Tbsp. of the batter into the center of the hot pan. Tilt the pan quickly toward you to cover the surface and cook until the batter forms tiny bubbles and begins to shrink from the outer edge of the pan. Tap the pan vigorously on the counter or loosen the crêpe with a spatula, allow it to slide half over the rim of the pan away from you and flip the pan to turn the crêpe. Cook for one minute longer, then slide the crêpe onto a turned-over saucer. After 12 to 15 crêpes have been made, oil the pan again, pour off the surplus and continue until all the batter is used up: it will make more crêpes than the 2 per person you will want to serve.

To prepare the chicken, put it in a large saucepan with the celery, carrot, onion, parsley, bay leaf, peppercorns and salt. Add cold water to cover, bring to a boil, then simmer, partially covered, for about an hour. Remove the chicken from the pot to cool. Strain the stock and set it aside to be used for soup or sauces—freeze it if you wish. When the chicken is cool enough to handle, skin it and remove the meat from the bones and chop it finely.

Heat the oven to 450°F.

To make the sauce, melt the butter in a heavy saucepan, add the flour and cook, stirring, for 2 or 3 minutes. Off the fire whisk in the milk, return to the fire and cook for 3 minutes more. Pour off one cup of the sauce, flavor it with salt, pepper and a good scraping of fresh nutmeg and mix it well with the chopped cooked chicken. Add the Parmesan cheese to the remaining 2 cups of sauce and cook, stirring, until it melts. Season liberally with salt and pepper.

To assemble the dish, place 2 Tbsp. of the cooked chicken mixture in the middle of a crêpe, roll it up and place the crêpes in a single row in a shallow buttered fireproof dish (use 1 large or as many smaller dishes as you need). Spoon enough of the sauce over the crêpes to coat them thoroughly. Put the dish in the 450° oven and bake for about 10 minutes, or until they are slightly browned on top and the sauce is bubbling. Keep an eye on them to prevent burning. Serve directly from the fireproof dish.

Strawberries Escoffier

    3 pints strawberries
    2 large oranges
    4 Tbsp. sugar
   ⅓ cup Grand Marnier or other orange liqueur
    1 cup heavy cream
    2 Tbsp. superfine sugar (optional)

Wash and hull the strawberries.

Grate both oranges, being careful not to include any of the white pith with the rind. Pound the sugar with the orange rind in a sturdy bowl, then squeeze the juice from the 2 oranges and pour it over the ·rind and sugar. Stir well and add the Grand Marnier.

Pour the Grand Marnier syrup over the strawberries and mix well. Allow them to marinate for at least an hour. The flavor will be more pronounced if the fruit is not refrigerated.

To whip the cream, pour it into a 2-quart bowl and leave it to chill in the freezer, if it will fit in, for 10 to 15 minutes (a bit longer in the refrigerator). Chill the beater or whisk. Add the fine sugar if you want, and beat until the cream is light and almost double its original volume. Serve the whipped cream in a separate dish.

SPRING DINNER

Sorrel Soup
Rack of Lamb Polynesian
Watercress Salad
Rhubarb Pie

Serves 6 to 8

Sorrel soup is no longer a familiar dish, but it is a splendid addition to a menu with fish, veal or lamb. Sorrel, sometimes called sourgrass, is a small spear-shaped leaf rather like dandelion which tastes sharp and refreshing. It's very rich in vitamins and minerals and is greatly prized by Jewish cooks as the chief ingredient in shav, a soup made from finely chopped sorrel mixed with sour cream. It is cultivated for sale but may be found growing wild in many parts of the United States; and although it may be purchased in bottles, I would advise you to wait for the fresh crop.

Buy very fresh leaves—although I doubt if you can do otherwise, since in large towns the addicts know where it can be bought and purchase the entire shipment soon after it is put on display. If you are fortunate enough to live in the country, identify the leaf from a wild plant booklet (it thrives in sandy soil), taste it to make sure you have the right one and pick it to your heart's content. Don't confine its use to soups—add sorrel to your green salads as well to give an extra fillip. Clean it away from the ribs and wash it as you would spinach to get rid of the sand and grit. And it must be cooked in stainless steel or enamel because its oxalic acid reacts with other metals to discolor the pan's contents.

The rack, or in French, carré of lamb is that part of the back which the rib chops come from. Left whole, it is a saddle, which you can locate by imagining where you would put a saddle on an animal; that portion of the animal, divided in half by cutting the backbone up the middle, is the rack. There should be no more than six or seven chops—beyond that you get into the loin chops. Most butchers will understand what you are after, although they may not know how to prepare it expertly for the oven. However, if a butcher asks if you want it frenched, the answer is yes; if he knows that much, the chances are he can do a passable job.

As there are only six to seven chops on the rack and I usually allow three chops a serving, for six servings you will need three racks, probably giving you a few extra chops as well. When you get the meat home, cut off all the fat. Don't be afraid to remove what looks like edible meat along with fat—it is edible, but not what we need for this dish. The rack should be trimmed right down to the solid meat called the eye. Scrape the chop bones clean of any fat or membrane and the rack is ready to be annointed with the basting sauce before being consigned to the oven. We will cook this for a short time in a hot oven.

I am never eager to serve a vegetable with the lamb, since I think it overcrowds the taste senses as well as the plate. The watercress, as much a garnish as a salad, is as far as I will go. You may yourself come to like the practice of not serving vegetables on the same plate as meat or fish, if you try it: I find it pleases the eye and the palate with its lack of confusion.

Rhubarb should be served early in the season in its youth. The stalks should be almost shocking pink and brittle. If they are inclined to limpness, repeat what I have prescribed in earlier chapters—cut the ends off the stalks and stand them in cold water for an hour or so. Don't forget that your vegetable is a living thing and may be extremely thirsty. Cut off the leaves, which are poisonous but which like most things in nature have their uses—boiled for ten minutes in water they are an effective spray against aphids and other plant pests.

I think rhubarb pie is all the better for being made beforehand and served at room temperature. Refrigeration does not improve pastry and there is little that can go wrong in the few hours between baking and serving.

Sorrel Soup

>   3 cups sorrel leaves, tightly packed
>   2 Tbsp. butter
>   6 cups chicken stock, of your own making
>   or a good, clear canned chicken broth,
>   heated to a boil
>   4 egg yolks
>   ¾ cup heavy cream
>   2 Tbsp. frozen green peas or lima beans,
>   puréed in a blender or by forcing
>   through a wire strainer (optional)
> Salt and freshly ground black pepper

Remove the midrib from the sorrel with a sharp knife and discard. Then wash the leaves in cold running water and drain. Chop finely and sauté in the melted butter until wilted—there will be only about 3 Tbsp. left. Add the hot chicken stock and simmer gently for a minute or so. Take off the heat. Beat the egg yolks in a small bowl, stir the cream into them and add very slowly to the sorrel and stock mixture, which should be hot but no longer boiling. Heat gently until the soup thickens, being careful not to let it boil, then add the purée of green peas or lima beans, if desired. Season to taste with salt and pepper.

Rack of Lamb Polynesian

>   3 racks of lamb
> Paper frills for the bone ends (optional)

Basting Sauce:

>   ½ clove garlic, crushed
>   ½ tsp. salt
>   2 Tbsp. dry mustard
>   2 Tbsp. olive oil
>   ¼ tsp. freshly ground black pepper
>   4 heaping Tbsp. dark brown sugar
>   2 Tbsp. soya sauce
>   ⅓ cup fresh lemon juice

Sprigs of watercress (optional)

To prepare the basting sauce, crush the garlic clove with the salt. Mix the dry mustard and olive oil to make a smooth paste. Add all the remaining ingredients and the garlic salt and mix thoroughly. This sauce is best made several hours before it is to be used.

Heat the oven to 425°F.

Cut all the fat from the racks of lamb and remove the layer of thin meat and fat that covers the eye—there should be nothing left but the eye clinging to the bone. Brush the sauce over the meat and arrange in a roasting pan—a metal rack is not needed, as the racks should be so arranged that they rest on the long bone with the eye of meat on top. Cook for 15 minutes, then brush again with the sauce. Cook for a further 15 minutes.

Once out of the oven, let the meat rest for 5 minutes to allow the juices to retreat from the surface. Carve the rack in single and double chops, allowing one of each per person. To serve, slip the bone of the single chop between the 2 bones of the double one and, if you like, put a paper frill on the end of the single chop bone. Arrange them on a heated platter and garnish with sprigs of watercress.

Watercress Salad

2 bunches fresh watercress
1 small head of Boston lettuce
1 mixing vinaigrette dressing (page 23)

Wash the watercress thoroughly and remove the coarse stems. Dry and store in plastic bags in the refrigerator until needed.

Wash and dry the lettuce. I use Boston or any other sturdy green lettuce to bolster up the watercress—it prevents the delicate watercress from collapsing completely after it has been dressed. Toss the greens with the vinaigrette dressing just before serving.

Rhubarb Pie

> 3 lbs. young pink rhubarb
> 2½ cups sugar
> ¼ tsp. ground ginger
> Rind of 1 lemon, grated
> 1 egg yolk mixed with 2 Tbsp. milk

Short Pastry (to be made 2 hours before needed):

> 3 cups all-purpose flour
> 3 level Tbsp. shortening
> ¼ lb. (1 stick) very cold butter
> 3 to 4 Tbsp. ice water
> ½ tsp. salt
>
> 1-quart pie dish, buttered
> Superfine sugar
> 1 cup heavy cream, whipped (optional)

To make the pastry, sift the flour into a mixing bowl. Add the shortening and chip the cold butter into the bowl. Break up with a pastry blender or 2 forks or your fingers until the mixture is coarse and mealy. (I use the tips of my fingers, which are cooler than the palms.) Add the water—3 Tbsp. is the least that will be needed and 4 the most. You want just enough water to enable you to form the dough into a ball, handling it as little as possible.

Smear the dough outward from the center of a floured board, using the heel of your hand with the weight of your body behind it. You are thus blending the flour, fats and moisture. Gather the dough back into a ball, seal in a plastic bag or wrap and refrigerate it for at least 2 hours.

In the meantime, prepare the rhubarb. Cut a slice off the top and bottom of the rhubarb stalk, making quite sure you have removed all the leaves. Cut the stalks into 1½- to 2-inch pieces. Mix the rhubarb, sugar, ground ginger and lemon rind in a bowl. Pile the rhubarb into the pie dish, mounding it high to form a dome.

Heat the oven to 350°F.

Take the pastry from the refrigerator and roll it out to a thickness of an ⅛ of an inch. Brush the edge of the pie dish with the egg yolk and milk mixture, then lay the pastry over the rhubarb in the pie dish. Cut it to fit with a sharp knife and press it firmly to the edge of the dish. Gather together what is left of the pasty and roll it out again. Cut strips about 1 inch wide and long enough to go around the circumference of the dish. Arrange the strips around the edge and press them firmly into place, then mark with a fork or with your fingers and thumb to form a hearty-looking edge. Brush the entire pastry dome with the egg mixture, then make cut-outs of the remaining pastry—leaves, strips or whatever takes your fancy—and press them into shape on the crust. Brush with the egg yolk once again. No steam vent is needed, as the rhubarb will hold the dough in place until it has been cooked. Bake for 1 hour in the 350° oven.

When it comes out of the oven, dust the pie at once with superfine sugar. Serve it hot, warm or at room temperature, with whipped cream if you like, but don't refrigerate it.

PICNIC

Quiche
Creamed Smoked Haddock
Tomato Salad
Two-Layer Biscuit
Fresh Fruit

Serves 6 to 8

I can never see any reason for a picnic to consist of thick unappetizing sandwiches munched in discomfort and washed down with some lukewarm liquid from a bottle or can. A picnic can have as much style and originality as any menu, and should be an occasion for having a meal one would be pleased to serve within the four walls of one's house.

Years ago a friend and I spent many a Saturday in early spring or late autumn motoring to out-of-the-way towns and villages in England, and we invariably brought a hot luncheon—perhaps creamed smoked haddock, which we both were fond of, cold vegetables, fresh crusty bread and cheese. A bottle of white wine which needed no chilling because of the time of the year, hot coffee and something to pick up with our fingers, small cakes or the like, and fresh fruit. The haddock we brought in a wide-mouthed thermos jug and ate on conventional plates rather than the paper imitation that bends alarmingly as soon as it receives its helping of food—although we did unbend and serve the wine in old horn drinking mugs. I go through the same ritual with friends now, going off to spots in woodlands or on the shore in very early spring when we will be untroubled by crowds. Modern technology has made the business of keeping foods hot or cold an easy matter, and we eat as well as ever. A cheese quiche has been added to my list of favorite picnic dishes, along with a simple salad of sliced tomatoes and a rich and crumbly sort of butterscotch biscuit with a coconut and pecan topping.

The smoked haddock you will find in a fish store, although it is now harder to come by than it was when smoked fish was standard fare in the British Isles and Scandinavia. The smoking industry has been practically strangled by frozen food packaging. But it is to me a great delicacy and well worth searching for.

The entire meal, with the exception of the sliced tomatoes, may be prepared the evening before the outing—I find that tomatoes are much too watery if sliced and dressed so far in advance, and it's only a matter of minutes to do them in the morning before setting out. Make the quiche the evening before, but do not refrigerate it. Prepare the haddock and its sauce at the same time, then in the morning reheat the sauce and stir in the fish before pouring it in its thermos. The fruit may be washed and refrigerated in the plastic bags in which you'll bring it, and white wine or soda refrigerated overnight. The biscuits can be done several days before if they are packed in an airtight tin, and you can make the hot coffee while you're having breakfast.

.I advise getting all the equipment together the previous day to make sure you don't have to dash to a store at the last minute for paper napkins or some such thing. With advance planning it takes little more than half an hour to pack up and go. Wipe off the wine bottles or cans and bottles of soft drinks and a container of drinking water and carry them in a cooler with ice. And don't forget the bottle opener and corkscrew. Bring rugs to sit on and, if you're willing to do things properly, a tablecloth; the paper substitute is an unnecessary economy. And set out with the intention of having a wonderful day.

Quiche

    Basic short pastry (page 72)
    9-inch glass or porcelain quiche or pie dish
      (I prefer to make the quiche in this type of
      dish rather than one from which it must be
      removed, as it is almost impossible to
      transport a free-standing pastry shell
      without smashing it to smithereens)
    1 egg white, lightly beaten

Filling:

    1¾ cups light cream or half-and-half
    1 cup sharp cheddar cheese, grated
    2 or 3 drops Tabasco sauce
    Freshly ground black pepper
    1 tsp. finely grated onion
    3 large eggs
    ½ cup Gruyère cheese in small dice

Prepare the pastry shell according to the directions on page 73.

To make the filling, bring the cream almost to the boil in a saucepan. Stir in the grated cheese and stir until it's melted. Add the Tabasco, pepper and grated onion. Beat the eggs lightly and stir them into the cream mixture. Pour this mixture into the baked shell and sprinkle the diced Gruyère evenly over the surface. It will sink out of sight, but don't let that worry you.

Bake for 40 minutes in the 325° oven, or until the custard is firm and the top lightly browned. The quiche should not be refrigerated but may be set aside uncovered overnight. It is ideally served at room temperature and so requires nothing more than gentle handling for serving at a picnic.

Creamed Smoked Haddock

 2 lbs. smoked haddock to make
  4 cups of cooked and flaked fish
Sufficient milk to cover
½ lb. small fresh mushrooms
3 Tbsp. butter
3 Tbsp. flour
Freshly ground black pepper

Soak the haddock in milk to cover for 1 hour, then bring the haddock and its milk slowly to a boil in a heavy pan. Allow it to cool, and, when the haddock is cool enough to handle, drain and reserve the milk in which it was cooked (you will need 2 cups of it further on). Remove the haddock's skin and all the bones.

Melt the 3 Tbsp. butter in a heavy pan and stir in the 3 Tbsp. flour. Cook gently for 2 or 3 minutes, being careful not to burn the roux. Heat 2 cups of the milk in which the haddock was cooked and, off the fire, pour it into the roux all at once. Whisk until smooth, return to gentle heat and cook for 5 or 6 minutes, stirring all the time. Correct the seasoning with the addition of freshly ground black pepper—you will find that extra salt will not be necessary. Wipe the mushrooms clean, cutting off the stems flush with the caps. If they are large, halve or quarter them: the pieces should be no larger than a quarter. Add them to the sauce and cook for 2 or 3 minutes more. Then refrigerate the sauce and fish separately if you are cooking them a night ahead, waiting until the morning to stir the flaked haddock into the sauce and heat them.

Tomato Salad

 5 to 6 tomatoes, not overripe
2¼ tsp. salt
2 tsp. sugar
2 Tbsp. lemon juice
4 Tbsp. oil, salad or olive
Freshly ground black pepper
½ cup parsley sprigs, chopped
4 or 5 sprigs fresh mint, chopped

Slice the tomatoes and lay them flat on a large platter or shallow dish. Sprinkle them with 2 tsp. of the salt and the 2 tsp. sugar and allow them to stand for half an hour.

Mix the lemon juice and oil together and add ¼ tsp. salt and 3 or 4 twists of the pepper mill. Sprinkle this over the tomatoes, then the chopped parsley and mint. The tomatoes should be packed in a polyethelene container.

Two-Layer Biscuit

Base:

    ½ cup butter
    1 cup flour
    1 cup brown sugar

Topping:

    ½ cup brown sugar
    2 eggs, beaten
    1 Tbsp. flour
    ½ cup grated coconut
    1 cup pecans
    Granulated sugar

Heat the oven to 375° F.

For the base, cream the butter, flour and brown sugar together until soft. Spread out carefully with the fingers on a 15¾ x 10½-inch baking sheet and bake for 15 minutes.

For the topping, mix carefully the ½ cup brown sugar, 2 beaten eggs, flour and coconut. Fold in the pecans. Pour this over the previously baked layer on the baking sheet and bake for 20 minutes in the 375° oven.

Sprinkle with granulated sugar immediately after removing from the oven and cut the biscuits while still warm, then store them in an airtight tin if they are not to be eaten right away.

SPRING BUFFET

Kedgeree of Salmon
Pollo Tonnato
Vegetable Salad   Salad of Bibb Lettuce
Cheese
Orange Cake

Serves 8 to 10

This menu is a delight on a warm spring day. If you are tempted, as I am, to spend more time out of doors with the return of temperate weather and longer daylight hours, most of the preparation may be done beforehand. And if you are fortunate enough to have a warm day for the affair, cool white wines may be served before, during and after the meal.

Don't be alarmed at sight of the salmon as a main dish—so little is needed that your purse will scarcely be aware of the cost. Kedgeree or Kegeree (I doubt if there is a correct spelling) is a dish which the British in India derived from the Indian Kitcheri. Kitcheri is made with rice and lentils and has no fish, but the British with their passion for smoked haddock used it in place of the lentils. On their return to the British Isles they introduced the dish they had rechristened Kedgeree to their countrymen, who promptly adopted it as well for salmon when it was in season. Soon no self-respecting Victorian breakfast sideboard was complete without it, as it took its place in the company of the devilled kidneys, kippers, ham, cold game and eggs of one sort or another which made up the run-of-the-mill English or Scottish country house breakfast of the late 19th and early 20th centuries. This breakfast of course preceded a day spent on the moors, on a reach of salmon river or riding to hounds. For our purposes, Kedgeree may be prepared well in advance and kept warm over hot water or in a mold in the oven.

Pollo Tonnato is a wonderfully elegant preparation of cold chicken, although you may very likely haul me over the coals for a breach in menu planning for including two rice dishes in the same meal. Let me assure you that they are both distinctive dishes making quite different uses of rice. The method for the Pollo was developed by my friend Helen McCully from the classic Vitello Tonnato and I am grateful to her for permission to use it.

A boiling hen is best suited for this dish, but if you can't find one, use two large roasting chickens. The boiler has the advantage of taking kindly to long slow cooking, and its stock is invaluable for soups and sauces as it turns to jelly when cool and freezes well.

The Pollo Tonnato may be assembled several hours before you wish to eat. The vegetable salad can be made at the same time and dressed half an hour before serving. Cheese should of course be taken out of the refrigerator several hours before you want to eat it. If your cheese man is reliable, he will tell you exactly when, expecially if you have a good Brie. The cake may be made at any time and frozen, if you wish. If frozen, it must be brought back to room temperature and doused again with orange and liqueur, then dusted with confectioner's sugar.

Kedgeree of Salmon

    1 lb. fresh salmon
    1 cup milk
    1 cup water
    2 tsp. salt
    4 cups cooked rice (1⅓ cups uncooked)
    2 Tbsp. butter, melted
    3 eggs, 2 boiled for 6 minutes,
        the third for 10 minutes
    Freshly ground black pepper
    ¼ tsp. imported curry powder
    2 Tbsp. finely chopped parsley

Pour the milk and water over the salmon in a heavy pan and add the salt.
Bring to a boil and simmer very gently for 10 minutes. Allow the salmon
to cool in the cooking liquid, then lift it out, reserving the liquid, and
remove all skin and bones. Flake the salmon, then mix it with the cooked
rice and melted butter in a bowl.

Shell the 2 6-minute boiled eggs and chop them finely. Stir them into the
rice mixture and season with 4 or 5 twists of the pepper mill and the curry
powder. Moisten with a little of the cooking liquid; the finished dish
should be moist, not dry and chewy—don't pour the cooking liquid out
until you're satisfied with the consistency of the rice and salmon. Taste for
seasoning. If the mixture needs a little more salt, this is the time to add it.

If the Kedgeree is to be served molded, pack it lightly into a buttered
2-quart mold, cover and keep it warm. Then turn it out to serve and
garnish it with chopped parsley and the shelled and chopped 10-minute
egg. Or it may be served simply spooned onto a platter.

Pollo Tonnato

    1 boiling fowl or 2 roasting chickens, totalling 6–7 lbs.
    1 7-oz. can tuna fish in oil
    1 small can flat anchovies, drained
    2 cups dry white wine
    ½ sour pickle

2   medium carrots, chopped
1   large onion, sliced
4   stalks celery, chopped
2   cloves garlic, finely chopped
1   small bunch parsley
16   peppercorns

2   cups long-grain rice
¾   cup parsley sprigs, chopped
2   Tbsp. capers, drained and chopped
Mayonnaise
Lemon juice
1   hardboiled egg

Put the fowl or chickens in a large pot with all the ingredients up to and including the 16 peppercorns. Cover with cold water and bring to a boil. Simmer gently until the fowl is cooked, which can be determined by testing the drumstick. If it moves freely, the bird is done. Cool it in the cooking liquid, then lift the fowl out of the pot and set it aside, but do not refrigerate it. Put the pot with the cooking liquid back on the stove and boil slowly until there are only about 2 to 2½ cups of liquid left. Strain through 3 thicknesses of moistened cheesecloth and reserve for making the finished sauce.

Cook the rice al dente and while it is cooling skin the chickens and remove and slice the meat from the legs and breast. Mix the rice with about ¾ of the chopped parsley, reserving the rest for garnishing the finished dish. Mound the rice on a suitable platter. Arrange the sliced chicken on top and sprinkle with the chopped capers.

The reduced cooking liquid should by now be on the point of setting. Mix this jelly with sufficient mayonnaise to make a sauce thick enough to adhere to the chicken when spooned over it—if it's too thin, it will run off. Season with lemon juice. This must be done to suit your taste but I suggest that it have a decided tang. Spoon the sauce over the sliced chicken to cover completely. Whatever sauce is left over should be served separately in a sauceboat.

Shell the hardboiled egg and put the yolk through a strainer or sieve with a wooden spoon. Decorate the border of the mounded chicken with a band of chopped parsley and another of the egg yolk. The dish may be assembled 2 hours or more before it is needed and refrigerated, but do not garnish with the egg and parsley until the last minute.

Vegetable Salad

2 carrots, peeled and sliced in matchsticks
1 lb. fresh green beans
1 9-oz. package frozen small lima beans
1 red onion, sliced in very thin rings
½ green pepper, thinly sliced
½ cucumber, thinly sliced
½ cup parsley sprigs, finely chopped
4 or 5 radishes, thinly sliced
2 tomatoes, each cut in 8 wedges
1 mixing vinaigrette dressing (page 23)
2 Tbsp. sour cream

Cook the carrots in boiling salted water for 2 or 3 minutes; they should remain crisp. Lift them out of the pot with a slotted spoon and cool them under cold running water. Cook the green beans in boiling salted water for 4 to 5 minutes, then drain and cool them. Cook the lima beans according to the package directions, drain and cool.

Put all the ingredients except the tomatoes in a large bowl. Add ½ cup vinaigrette dressing plus the 2 Tbsp. sour cream and mix well. Garnish with the tomato wedges.

Salad of Bibb Lettuce

4 to 5 heads of Bibb lettuce
1 mixing vinaigrette dressing

Wash the lettuce in several changes of water, then drain and dry it carefully. Toss lightly with the dressing.

The cheeses I'd suggest to go with this menu are Brie, Port de Salut and Gorgonzola Colombo.

Orange Cake

> Butter and sugar for lining the baking pan
> 16 Tbsp. (2 sticks) unsalted butter
> 1 cup sugar
> 3 large eggs, separated
> 2 cups all-purpose flour
> 1 tsp. baking powder
> 1 tsp. baking soda
> 1 cup sour cream
> Grated rind of 1 orange
> ½ cup chopped nuts (walnuts, pecans or hazelnuts)
> ¼ cup fresh orange juice
> ⅓ cup Grand Marnier, Cointreau or other orange liqueur
> Confectioner's sugar

Heat the oven to 350° F.

Prepare an 8- or 9-inch spring form or tube pan by buttering the inside and dusting it with sugar, shaking out any that has not stuck to the butter.

Cream together the butter and sugar until light and pale yellow. Beat in the egg yolks. Sift the flour, baking powder and baking soda together and add them to the butter, sugar and egg mixture alternatively with the sour cream, stirring until smooth. Stir in the orange rind and the chopped nuts. Beat the egg whites until stiff but not dry and fold them into the batter. Spoon the mixture into the pan and cook for 45 to 50 minutes or until the inserted blade of a knife comes out clean.

Mix the orange juice and liqueur and spoon over the cake while it is still hot. Cool before removing it from the pan. Dust the top with confectioner's sugar. If the cake is not to be used right away, store it in an airtight tin or in a plastic bag. I will admit to spooning a little more orange and liqueur mixture over the cake just before serving if it was made beforehand.

❧ SUMMER ☙

The summer of the Northern Hemisphere sneaks up on one. Spring seems suddenly to have been an unfinished rehearsal, culminating in an ungainly rush to dust off garden furniture and make ready the outdoor broiler or, for the city dweller, to plant petunias in window boxes and resign oneself largely to top-of-the-stove cooking. But in the city or the country, we must face the common task of planning menus to suit the season.

All too often hot-weather meals consist of salads and long, cool drinks. This is all very well when not overdone, but I have never considered frosted pitchers of lemonade and trembling jellies the epitome of summer fare. Energy-giving foods are just as necessary in the heat of summer as in winter, perhaps more so, since on the whole we lead more active lives when out of doors. Rather than cutting down on the amount of food to be served in hot weather, make an effort to vary it and devote some attention to its presentation: in order to tempt us despite the heat, summer foods must appeal both to the eye and the palate.

Summer fare that is both nutritious and enticing includes poached fish with light sauces, poultry dishes, mousses and fruit desserts. Highly spiced dishes may be quite refreshing to the palate, as with the Vindaloo soup, which takes its name from a type of Indian curry. Cold soups are legion and make excellent first courses. If you have a freezer there is little excuse for neglecting to keep frozen stock for use as a soup base. The blender, an invention I consider one of the best since the wheel, takes the back-breaking work out of soupmaking and is to my mind an essential household acquisition. Salads need not be confined to green leaves and a dressing—what the French call the Salade Composée gives endless scope for improvisation.

There is no need for devoted outdoor cooks to confine themselves to broiled steak, chicken and fish. Paella can be cooked over charcoal and is a wonderful dish to prepare before the fascinated eyes of your guests outdoors. The single secret of its success is the meticulous preparation and organization of its many ingredients. And there is of course the wonderful repertory of ices and ice creams which may be expanded as far as your imagination will take you.

SUMMER LUNCHEON

Vindaloo Soup
Roulade of Crab with Mayonnaise Mousseline
Salad of Petits Pois
Fresh Peach Compote

Serves 8

The ideal summer luncheon, to my way of thinking, is light and can be prepared in advance. I am particularly fond of this menu, which fulfills both these requirements.

The Vindaloo is a particularly light, non-fattening soup which may be served hot or cold. Cool and spicy, it will act as an aperitif to sharpen your guests' appetites.

The Roulade of Crab is quite easy to make and sufficiently unusual to arouse your guests' admiration. Smoked haddock may be substituted for the crab, as it was in the small London restaurant where I first had this dish. I have also at times used lobster meat and served the roulade hot with Sauce Nantua, although I don't do this often because of the cost and the inconvenience of having to serve it hot.

I would suggest you buy the best quality pasteurized crab meat. Make the roulade several hours before it is to be used, but don't refrigerate it. It doesn't freeze at all well, so don't make the attempt.

Buy the best brand of small frozen peas for the salad. To cook, no matter what the package instructions are, drop them into boiling salted water and drain after one minute. Use small white onions very thinly sliced. To remove their skins, drop the onions into boiling water, count to ten and drain them. When cool enough to handle they may be squeezed out of their skins after the root end has been cut off. Dress the salad with vinaigrette dressing to which chopped fresh mint has been added. There should be no problem finding fresh mint in summer: most of us who have gardens find it a menace that needs strict controlling. Or a pot can be successfully cultivated on a terrace; a little goes a long way.

Shop for locally grown peaches—and by that I mean peaches that have been tree-ripened. They should be available at this time of year. Make the simple syrup beforehand and chill it. To peel the peaches, drop them into

95

boiling water for about ten seconds, drain and if they are in good condition the skin will peel off without difficulty. Cut them in half and remove the stone, then quarter and pour the syrup over them immediately. This prevents their discoloring. You may want to add extra sugar, but I don't recommend the addition of liqueur of any kind as this detracts from the freshness of the fruit.

Vindaloo Soup

    5 ribs celery
    6 carrots
    6 cups beef or chicken stock
    Rind of ½ lemon, chopped fine
    2 Tbsp. tomato purée
    2 tsp. imported curry powder
    ½ cup dry white vermouth
    Salt and pepper
    1½ Tbsp. finely chopped parsley

Wash the celery and carrots. Peel the carrots, and chop coarsely 4 of the carrots and 3 ribs of celery, putting the chopped vegetables in a heavy 2-quart pot with a lid and setting aside the remaining 2 carrots with 2 ribs of celery. Add the stock to the pot and simmer gently, covered, for half an hour. Strain, reserving the stock, and purée the cooked vegetables with the chopped lemon rind in a blender (or rub through a fine strainer). Add a little stock to help in the blending process.

Put the purée of vegetables back in the pot with the stock and add the tomato purée. Dice the remaining 2 carrots and 2 ribs of celery very finely and add them to the pan. Stir in the curry powder and dry vermouth. Heat gently for 5 to 6 minutes and season to taste with salt and pepper. Sprinkle with finely chopped parsley just before the soup is brought to the table, and serve either hot or cold.

Roulade of Crab

    1 lb. crabmeat
    8 eggs
    ⅔ cup lightly packed grated Parmesan cheese
    3 cups béchamel sauce
    Salt and pepper
    16 eggs, hardboiled and finely chopped

Béchamel Sauce:

> 8 Tbsp. butter
> 10 Tbsp. flour
> 4 cups milk
> Salt and freshly ground black pepper
> Scraping of nutmeg
> 2 Tbsp. anchovy paste

Heat the oven to 400° F. and line a flat 12- x 18-inch baking sheet with buttered greaseproof paper.

To prepare the béchamel sauce, melt the butter in a heavy 2-quart pot and stir in the flour. Cook gently, being careful not to burn. Heat the milk and add it all at once to the roux, and whisk until smooth. Cook slowly, stirring constantly, for 5 to 6 minutes. Season with salt and pepper and a scraping of nutmeg—the sauce should have a distinct flavor of nutmeg and should be thick and creamy enough to drop from a spoon. Stir in the 2 Tbsp. anchovy paste.

Add 1 cup of the sauce to the crabmeat. Separate the 8 eggs and beat the yolks into the crabmeat with 1/3 of the cheese. Beat the egg whites until firm but not dry and fold them into the crab mixture with a large metal spoon. Spread this mixture evenly over the baking sheet. Bake on the top shelf of the oven for 10 to 15 minutes, or until well risen and firm to the touch.

Have ready a large sheet of greaseproof paper sprinkled with the remainder of the cheese. Quickly turn the roulade onto this and strip off the paper on which it was baked. Add the finely chopped hardboiled eggs to the remaining sauce and spread over the roulade. Trim the sides, then tilt the paper and roll up as you would a jelly roll. Serve hot or cold with the mayonnaise mousseline served separately in a sauceboat.

Mayonnaise Mousseline

    4 egg whites
    Salt and pepper
    2 Tbsp. lemon juice
    2 Tbsp. finely chopped parsley
    2 cups mayonnaise

Mayonnaise:

    6 egg yolks
    ½ tsp. French Dijon mustard
    Salt and pepper
    2 cups olive oil
    2 Tbsp. (approximately) lemon juice or wine vinegar

To make the mayonnaise, place a mixing bowl on a wet towel to hold it steady, and put into it the egg yolks, mustard and a pinch each of salt and pepper. Beat the mixture well with a wire whisk or wooden spoon. Add about 2 Tbsp. of the oil, a drop at a time, while continuing to whisk. As the oil is absorbed gradually add the remainder. If it becomes too thick, add a little lemon juice or vinegar to thin. Correct the seasoning. It may be stored for as long as 3 days in the refrigerator.

For the mayonnaise mousseline, beat the 4 egg whites with a pinch of salt until they stand in stiff peaks. Add the lemon juice and more salt and pepper to the 2 cups of mayonnaise, mixing well. Fold the egg whites into the mayonnaise and sprinkle with the finely chopped parsley.

Salad of Petits Pois

    2 small white onions
    2 10-oz. packages frozen petits pois
    1 mixing vinaigrette dressing (page 23)
    1 Tbsp. chopped mint leaves

Drop the onions into a pan of boiling water for 10 seconds, then drain, cut off the root ends, squeeze off the skins and slice very thinly. Plunge the frozen peas into a quantity of boiling salted water for 1 minute only, then drain.

Toss the onions and peas with the vinaigrette dressing to which 1 Tbsp. chopped mint has been added.

Fresh Peach Compote

    2 cups sugar
    4 cups water
    1 lemon, sliced
    8 peaches, tree-ripened

Make a syrup by combining the sugar, water and lemon slices in a saucepan. Bring the syrup to a boil and boil it for 3 minutes. Let it cool and chill it slightly.

Drop the peaches into boiling water for 10 seconds, then take them out with a slotted spoon, drain and remove the skin when they're cool enough to handle. Cut the peaches in half to remove the stones, then into quarters or eighths. Spoon the syrup over the peaches carefully and set them aside until you're ready to serve them. In my opinion they have a better flavor if they're not refrigerated.

SUMMER DINNER

Summer Squash Soup
Roast Chicken
Mélange of Vegetables   Watercress Salad
Strawberry Meringue Torte

Serves 6 to 8

At first sight this menu appears very simple and unsophisticated. It is both and that's why I like it.

The soup is something a child can put together. It is rich and creamy without a trace of cream, and it is subtle.

As for the chicken, once you have roasted one by this method I doubt if you will ever resort to any other. Once it's ready for the oven it needs no further attention, and turns out moist, crisp-skinned and bursting with flavor. It is equally good cold, and in fact I often serve it with a salad for luncheon at room temperature, never just out of the refrigerator. And it's ideal for cholesterol-conscious people—no fats of any kind are added and the lemon juice cuts whatever fat there is in the chicken itself.

The chicken should be fresh—and by that I mean not frozen—and weigh not less than three pounds; three and a half is ideal. (Chickens under three pounds seem to me to have as much bone as the larger ones, so why not opt for more meat.)

I garnish the plate with a mixture of available vegetables, and at this time of year there are many—carrots, fresh green beans, new peas and small cauliflowers. All together they make a good-looking picture. The vegetables may be cooked beforehand and heated in butter or oil before serving. I have used watercress salad again because I can't think of any green salad that goes better with this roast chicken.

The torte may be made the day of the dinner, or the meringue may be made as much as a week before and stored in an airtight tin box. Whichever, it can be put together an hour or so before dinner and kept in the refrigerator.

I find that meringue may be most successfully cooked or, to be accurate, dried out in a 250° oven for one hour, with the heat then turned off and the meringue left in the oven overnight. This produces the crunchy meringue which is needed for the torte. On some other occasion you might want to try to alternate method of putting the meringues in an oven preheated to 475° F. and turning off the heat immediately, again leaving them overnight: this results in a chewy meringue.

If the cream is sufficiently heavy, the torte will not get soggy. The strawberries must be dried thoroughly after they are washed and hulled, then dusted with sugar. I can't specify the amount of sugar to be used—that depends on you and the strawberries.

Summer Squash Soup

    2 medium yellow summer squash
    2 small green zucchini
    1½ cups celery leaves
    3 Tbsp. butter
4 6 cups chicken stock
       Salt (and celery salt, if possible)
       Pepper
    2 Tbsp. finely chopped parsley

Wash but do not peel the summer squash and zucchini. Chop into small pieces; do not remove the seeds. In a covered pan, cook the summer squash and zucchini with the celery leaves in the 3 Tbsp. butter over very low heat until tender (approximately 6 or 7 minutes). Purée the mixture in a blender, adding a little of the chicken stock to assist in blending. Mix this purée with the remaining stock.

Correct seasoning by adding celery salt, salt and pepper. Serve hot or cold, garnished with finely chopped parsley.

Roast Chicken

    2 3-3½ pound roasting chickens
    2 cloves of garlic, peeled
       Juice of 2 lemons
       Coarse salt
       Freshly ground black pepper

Heat the oven to 400° F.

For each chicken: wipe the chicken inside and out with a clean cloth or paper towel. Sprinkle the inside very generously with salt and dust with freshly ground pepper (I have no hesitation in using a tablespoon of salt). Rub the inside with the garlic clove. Make a very thorough job of this. You will find that the salt acts as an abrasive so that a considerable amount of the garlic can be rubbed onto the chicken. Dust the outside with salt and repeat the garlic-rubbing operation, being careful to cover the entire surface of the chicken. If you are using an average clove of garlic most of it should have been rubbed off on the chicken by now.

Either truss the birds or fold the wing tips under the body and tie the legs securely to make a neat package. Squeeze the lemons and pour half inside each bird and the other half over the breast, spreading it evenly with your fingers. Dust once again with salt and freshly ground pepper.

Place the chickens on a rack in a roasting pan and pour a little water in the pan—this prevents the juices from burning. Put them in the oven, close the door and leave for 1 hour. Basting is not needed. Once out of the oven, allow the chickens to rest in a warm spot for 5 or 10 minutes. Pour the pan juices over the birds before carving.

Mélange of Vegetables

        3 carrots
        3 ribs celery
        1 lb. fresh green beans
        ¼ lb. fresh mushrooms
        3 Tbsp. butter
        2 Tbsp. oil, olive or vegetable
        2 tsp. fresh lemon juice
        ½ tsp. sugar
        Salt and freshly ground black pepper
        2 Tbsp. finely chopped parsley

Wash and scrape the carrots, using a vegetable peeler. Cut off both ends and slice on the bias, about ¼-inch thick. Wash the celery and remove the fibrous outside with the vegetable peeler, then slice on the bias to the same thickness as the carrots.

Wash the green beans and cut off the ends with scissors—the fastest way to do it, I find. Bring 1 quart of water to a boil in a heavy pan, then add the beans and 2 Tbsp. of salt. Bring to the boil once again and cook for 2 minutes only. Drain and run under cold water to prevent further cooking and set them aside.

Wipe the mushrooms with a damp cloth. Cut the ragged ends from the stalks, then slice the mushrooms very thinly and set them aside. Squeeze the lemon juice and have the other seasonings ready.

Heat a large heavy pan capable of holding 3 to 4 quarts; if you are the proud owner of a wok, use it. I also find an electric skillet most suitable for stir frying, which indeed this is. Add the butter and oil and allow them to melt. Add the carrots, stir to coat well with butter and oil and cook for 3 to 4 minutes, stirring. Add the celery and cook for another 2 minutes; then add the beans and lastly the mushrooms. Cook for 2 minutes and add the lemon juice and sugar. Stir well and season to taste with salt and freshly ground black pepper.

The times given are approximate. Use your judgment to decide whether you want your vegetables al dente or well cooked. Stir in the chopped parsley just before serving.

Strawberry Meringue Torte

    8 egg whites (approximately 1 cup)
    Pinch of salt
    ½ tsp. cream of tartar
    2 cups superfine sugar
    1 quart fresh strawberries
    2 cups heavy cream
    Sugar for sweetening
    Confectioner's sugar

Heat the oven to 225° F.

Line 2 cookie sheets without raised edges with parchment paper or brown paper, which helps diffuse the heat, and mark 2 eight-inch circles on each sheet with a pencil. Set aside till the meringue is ready.

Leave the egg whites in the refrigerator for 20 minutes, then beat them till they're foaming. Add the salt and cream of tartar and continue beating until stiff. At this point start adding the sugar gradually, beating continually. If you are using an electric mixer pour it in slowly and continuously, otherwise spoon it in by hand. Continue beating until the mixture is heavy, smooth and has a definite shine.

If you are handy with a pastry bag fitted with a star tube, fill in the marked circles with the mixture. It should be possible to divide the mixture in 4 equal parts by eye. If you can't cope with a pastry bag, spoon the meringue over the circles, smoothing it with a damp palette knife before putting it in the oven. Bake for 1 hour and turn off the heat. If you are in a hurry leave the door open, allowing the meringues to cool, but if you can afford the time leave them in the oven all night. Always allow meringues to cool away from a draft. If they must be stored, keep them in an air-tight tin—they absorb moisture like sponges and break up as a result.

Wash the strawberries and remove the hulls. Pick out 6 or 8 of the best-looking and slice the others. If they are sour, as is often the case, dust them with fine sugar to taste and let them stand for 10 or 15 minutes. Whip the cream until it holds definite peaks when the beater is lifted. If the strawberries have been sweetened I don't add sugar to the cream, but this is very much a matter of taste—if you think it is needed, go ahead and add sugar while the cream is being whipped. Fold the sliced strawberries into the whipped cream.

To put the torte together, look carefully at the 4 meringue circles and set aside the best-looking one for the top. Put one ring on the serving plate and spoon whipped cream and strawberries onto it, keeping them away from the edge. Put the second ring on top of that and continue until all 4 have been used. Arrange the whole strawberries you have saved on top of the torte and dust with confectioner's sugar just before serving—if the sugar is added too soon it will be absorbed by the moist strawberries.

TERRACE SUPPER

Cheese Tart
Paella
Salad Bagatelle Coffee Ice Cream

Serves 8

The terrace or garden meal can be great fun, provided that you do not have the mistaken impression that it is an easy way to cook and entertain. It is not. But cooking and eating out of doors, however limited your outdoor circumstances, is a welcome change from working over a hot oven. Another possible advantage is that most American men take pride in their prowess at cooking over charcoal, and might be more than willing to attempt such a spectacular dish as the paella, which is not difficult, although it demands the cook's unswerving attention.

My first rule on outdoor meals is not to invite too many people, since adequate seating and room to move about are essential to everyone's comfort. Have a table for drinks handy, if possible, and the charcoal broiler at a distance. I would advise the cook to have water at hand for damping down the charcoal fire—paella needs a gentle heat or it is made tough and dry.

Make the cheese tart or tarts in the morning, but don't refrigerate them. Cut them in small slices to be picked up in the fingers, which will cut down on the washing up.

Prepare the salad ingredients early in the day and refrigerate them. Have the dressing ready and take it out of the refrigerator half an hour before it's needed. Mix and dress the salad well when the paella is nearly ready. They may be served on the same plate.

Have all the ingredients for the paella ready on a tray in the order in which they are to be used. Once it is put together, all you have to do is keep an eye on the charcoal to make sure it is not going too fast.

The ice cream may be made in the morning or while your party is in progress. Personally, I like to finish it early in the day and refrigerate the container or pack it in ice. The noise of an electric ice cream-maker cranking away drives me to distraction and is certainly not conducive to good conversation. I'd suggest serving ice cream in shallow glass bowls or old-fashioned glasses—this should spare your guests from having to chase a ball of ice cream around a plate with a spoon.

Finally, before retiring for the night make sure the charcoal fire has been quenched.

Cheese Tart

Pastry:

    3 cups flour, sifted
    1 tsp. salt
    6 oz. (12 Tbsp.) unsalted butter
    6 Tbsp. ice water
    2 8- or 9-inch flan rings or tart tins

Filling:

    4 Tbsp. butter
    4 Tbsp. flour
    1 cup milk
    4 oz. grated Gruyère cheese
    2 oz. grated Parmesan cheese
    Freshly grated nutmeg
    Salt and pepper
    2 eggs, separated

Heat the oven to 400° F.

To make the pastry, sift the flour and salt together. Crumble the butter into the sifted flour, then add the ice water a little at a time while mixing with a fork or pastry cutter. Form into a ball, handling the dough gently and using no more pressure than necessary to make it hold together. Allow it to rest for an hour in plastic wrap in the refrigerator.

Divide the dough into 2 equal pieces and press each into a flan ring or tart tin, using your knuckles and fingers—this handling takes the place of rolling. Allow a little to hang over the edge of the tin. Prick the bottom of the pastry with a fork and fit a piece of foil over the bottom surface and up the sides (this is to prevent the pastry from rising and being contorted out of shape). Bake for 30 minutes in the middle of the preheated oven. The shells or cases may be baked the day before or even further ahead and frozen.

For the filling, melt the butter in a heavy pan and allow it to cook without changing color for 1 or 2 minutes. This is to evaporate any water that may be in the butter. Stir in the flour and cook gently for 3 or 4 minutes, being careful not to burn the roux. If the flour and butter mixture is not sufficiently cooked at this stage, it will be almost impossible to get rid of the floury taste that is so often in evidence in badly made sauces. Heat the milk until it is hot but not boiling. Pour it all at once into the flour and butter and stir vigorously with a wire whisk. If the pan is heavy, it will have retained enough heat to thicken the sauce. Return the pan to the stove and cook gently for 3 or 4 minutes, stirring. Stir in ¼ tsp. grated nutmeg—a little more will be needed, but this is enough for the present. Cool the mixture slightly and stir in the grated cheeses. Correct the seasoning with additional nutmeg if you think it is needed, and freshly ground pepper and salt. We have not added salt until now because the cheese may be salty and one cannot judge until it has been added. Allow the mixture to cool.

Beat the egg yolks and stir them into the cheese mixture. Beat the whites till they hold definite peaks, then fold them gently but firmly into the mixture and spoon it into the shells. Bake for 15 minutes in a 400° oven. The top should be rich and brown and the center still slightly creamy.

Salad Bagatelle

> 12 medium carrots
> 1 lb. mushrooms
> 2 lbs. asparagus
> 3 sticks celery
> 1 cup parsley sprigs, coarsely chopped
> 1 mixing vinaigrette dressing (page 23)

Have 2 quarts water and 2 Tbsp. salt at a rolling boil. Wash and peel the carrots, then slice and cut them into matchsticks. Drop them into the boiling salted water. As soon as the water comes back to the boil, lift the carrots out (reserving the water) and run cold tap water over them until they are cool.

Remove the mushroom stems by cutting them off flush with the caps. Wipe them clean with a damp towel or paper, then slice very thin.

Cut the tips from the 2 lbs. of asparagus. Wash in cold water to remove any grains of sand. Bring the carrot water to a boil again and put in the asparagus tips. Bring back to a boil and cook for 1 minute, then test them. The tips should be still crisp. If they're not sufficiently done, cook for 1 more minute. Drain and rinse under cold running water.

Wash the celery and if it is not young and tender, remove the outside fiber with a vegetable peeler. Slice very thinly on the bias.

Mix all these ingredients and the chopped parsley in the salad bowl, then cover and refrigerate until an hour or so before serving time. Take the salad out of the refrigerator and toss it with the vinaigrette half an hour before the meal. Taste for seasoning—more salt and pepper may be needed.

Paella

> 1 small chicken weighing about 2 lbs.,
>   cut in 16 pieces
> 18 shrimp
> 3 medium tomatoes
> 24 green beans
> 4 oz. salt pork
> 2 chorizo sausages
> 1 small green pepper
> ½ cup green peas
> 4 to 6 Tbsp. olive oil
> Salt and freshly ground black pepper
> 2 tsp. paprika
> 5 cups water
> ½ tsp. saffron
> 2 cups rice, preferably long-grain

I find the preparations for making paella very similar to those for Chinese or Japanese cooking—that is, all three depend on ordering the ingredients so that they may be combined for cooking with great rapidity. This requires the use of your visual sense, to which you should give free reign—and your guests will be charmed to see the quantity of carefully arranged ingredients and their incorporation into the finished dish. Prepare all the ingredients on good-looking trays or platters and arrange them in the order in which they are to be used. This is the time-consuming part of the venture, not the actual cooking, and it is absolutely crucial to the success of your paella, since during the cooking itself you will need to devote your attention to keeping the fire at a gentle level and to carefully managing the timing of the whole enterprise.

The paella pan should be about 2 inches deep and 12 in diameter and hold 8 to 10 cups. It may be made of earthenware, iron or aluminum: An earthenware pan is fine if you take extra care in controlling the heat and when cleaning it and it works well on charcoal. However, I find that the aluminum pan is better for practical reasons. It may be bought in shops that sell cooking equipment and in houseware departments of department stores. If you don't own one of these, a large skillet will do. But don't put off making the paella just because you don't have the called-for utensil: try to fashion some substitute. The basic requirement is a large flat surface, since the rice and other ingredients need to be spread out, not piled up.

If the butcher has not cut up the chicken for you, cut off the legs and divide the thigh from the drumstick—this will give you 4 pieces. Cut off the wings by slicing along the breast from back to neck, taking some of the breast with the knife—with a little maneuvering of the knife it should not be too difficult to find the joint that holds the wing to the body. Now there are 6 pieces. Divide the breast in 2 with the bone—that makes 8. With a cleaver cut each piece in half again, making 16 in all. The back does not provide much meat but will yield a quart of good chicken stock for future use.

Peel the shrimp and with a small sharp knife slit each along the back and remove the small dark vein (there will often not be one visible). Wash under cold running water.

Bring a small pan of water to a boil and drop the tomatoes in one at a time and count 10. Lift them out with a slotted spoon. With a small knife remove the stalk end and peel. It will come away easily. Cut each tomato in quarters and chop rather coarsely.

Top and tail the beans (cut off each end) and cut in 1-inch pieces. Cut the salt pork in ½-inch dice, the sausages in ½-inch slices. Slice the pepper in half and remove the white pith and all the seeds—the latter is important as the seeds are hot and will unbalance the finished flavor of the paella. Cut the pepper in strips and then in 1-inch pieces. Have the shelled green peas near at hand.

We are now ready to cook. Heat 4 Tbsp. of the oil in the pan over moderate heat. Dust the chicken pieces with salt and freshly ground black pepper. Cook them gently in the oil for about 12 minutes until they are golden brown—concentrate mostly on the skin side. Remove the chicken pieces and set aside on a plate. In the same oil, fry the diced salt pork for 3 minutes, then add the chopped tomato. Stir in the paprika and cook a minute or 2 longer. Add the 5 cups of hot water. Put back the chicken pieces and simmer for 10 minutes.

Take out ¼ cup of the hot liquid and soak the saffron in it for about 15 minutes. Add the rice, shrimp, sausage, green beans and green pepper to the pan, stir with a fork and cook gently but steadily for 15 minutes. Strain the saffron liquid and add it to the pan, stir briefly and cook for a further 6 to 7 minutes, when the rice should be cooked, but do not stir during this time. Test a grain or two of the rice in your teeth, and if it is not sufficiently cooked, leave the pan on the heat a little longer. If the water has evaporated, add a little more; if there is too much water just before the rice is finished, increase the heat and cook quickly until the rice is finally dry. Each grain should be separate and golden yellow.

Correct the seasoning by adding salt and pepper to taste. You may stir once again with a fork to mix the rice and additional seasonings. Serve the paella from the pan in which it has been cooked. Traditionally it is eaten with a spoon—knives and forks are considered an unnecessary refinement.

Serve with a mixed green salad of your choice.

Coffee Ice Cream

    ½ cup sugar
    4 egg yolks
    ⅛ tsp. salt
    2 cups milk (scalded)
    1 envelope unflavored gelatin, sprinkled over
       ¼ cup water

2½ Tbsp. instant coffee
1 cup heavy cream
1 tsp. brandy
Electric ice-cream maker

Beat the sugar, egg yolks and salt until lemon-colored. Add the scalded milk and cook very gently over low heat in a heavy pan till it coats the back of a spoon. Strain if necessary, then add the softened gelatin. Add the coffee and set aside to cool. When the mixture has cooled completely, add the heavy cream and brandy.

Pour this mixture into the canister of an electric ice-cream maker and pack it with 3 cups of ice for each cup of coarse salt, packing the ice and salt in alternate layers. Freeze for a maximum of 45 minutes, but check after 25 minutes.

SUMMER BUFFET

Poached Sea Trout   Navarin of Lamb
New Potatoes in Mint Vinaigrette
Raspberry Sorbet   A Small Chocolate Cake
                                    Serves 12 to 14

The dishes for this summer buffet make a colorful and varied table, offering a wealth of choice to people who love to eat good food and at the same time providing an opportunity for the weight-conscious to pick their way carefully and still dine well. And there is no reason for last-minute scrambling, as all the preparation and cooking are completed much ahead of time.

Viewing the menu through the other end of the telescope, the small chocolate cake may be made several days or a week before and frozen. So may the sorbet. The Navarin of Lamb can be cooked the day before; in fact, it is better when left to settle. This leaves you with only the sea trout and the potatoes to cook in the morning.

Sea trout (called weakfish by East Coast fishermen because of its inability to hold the hook firmly) is in season from May until October. I consider it a great delicacy because of its very tender flesh, and any sauce you may ever think of serving with it should complement rather than mask its flavor. For a party of ten to fourteen, I prefer to serve two four- to five-pound fish rather than one very large one. When the first has been devoured it is satisfying to have a second, completely intact, to take its place.

As for all poaching, the court bouillon should be prepared some time before it is to be used to allow the herbs and spices to produce an aromatic liquid; there should be enough to cover the fish in its pan or kettle, the name given the long, narrow pan which the French developed for cooking fish. One of France's authorities on fish has defined poaching as cooking in a liquid "just gently trembling so that cooking proceeds by a gradual penetration of heat into the fish"—too rapid boiling will cause the fish to break up. The fish should be left in its kettle to cool so that it may absorb as much as possible of the court bouillon. When it's cool enough to

121

handle, remove the skin but leave the head on. The fish is best served at room temperature.

Make the Navarin of Lamb the day before. Cool thoroughly before refrigerating and, before reheating, take off any fat that is visible. If the lamb has been prepared carefully, there should be little. When reheating, do so gently. It is always better to use low heat and allow more time than to do it quickly with high heat. I find a 325° oven suitable.

If you are fortunate enough to find really new potatoes that slide out of their skins, do little more than wash them. If they are older, peel them carefully. Mint is plentiful and inexpensive, so put two or three sprigs in the cooking water. Dress the potatoes with the vinaigrette while they are still warm and sprinkle with chopped mint before serving. I would advise you not to refrigerate them.

If the chocolate cake has been frozen, take it out the evening before and put it in the refrigerator. It should be served at room temperature, and you will need to allow it 2 to 3 hours out of the refrigerator to achieve this. If you don't want to frost it, a dusting of confectioner's sugar is sufficient and looks good.

An hour before the party, spoon the sorbet into a glass bowl and put it back in the freezer. If you want to serve it spectacularly, stand the bowl in a larger one full of cracked ice on the buffet.

Poached Sea Trout

    4 quarts of water
    1 bay leaf
    1 medium-sized carrot, chopped coarsely
    3 to 4 ribs of celery, chopped
    1 small onion stuck with 3 cloves
    2 Tbsp. salt
    2 cups dry white wine
    1 small bunch of parsley
    6 peppercorns
    2 sea trout, each weighing as close to 5 lbs.
       as possible
    1 cucumber, sliced
    Sprigs of parsley
    Sprigs of watercress

Put the water and all the ingredients except the trout, cucumber, parsley and watercress, in a pan large enough to hold the fish. Bring to a boil and simmer covered for half an hour to infuse the liquid.

Ask your fishmonger to scale and clean the trout, leaving the heads on. Bring the court bouillon to a boil again, add the fish and reduce the heat so that the court bouillon just simmers or shivers. Cook for 20 minutes, then allow the fish to cool in the liquid. (Cooking times are approximately 15 minutes for 4 lbs., 20 minutes for 5 to 6 lbs., and 30 minutes for 8 to 10 lbs.) After the fish have cooled, take them out and very carefully remove the skin and the layer of dark colored flesh, which is fat—there is nothing harmful in the fat, but it looks gray and unappetizing. Arrange the fish on a long platter and decorate with slices of cucumber and sprigs of parsley and watercress. If you are handy with a pastry bag, use it to decorate the platter with rosettes of mayonnaise.

Don't put both fish on the buffet at the same time—the second may be produced to good effect after the first has been completely consumed. The court bouillon may be frozen and used again.

Navarin of Lamb

> 6 lbs. lean shoulder of lamb
> 6 Tbsp. olive oil
> 2 Tbsp. sugar
> Coarse salt and freshly ground black pepper
> 5 Tbsp. flour
> 4 tomatoes, peeled and chopped
> 3 cloves garlic, crushed
> ½ tsp. dry thyme
> 1 bay leaf
> 5 cups stock made from lamb bones or 5 cups
>   canned chicken consommé
> 8 carrots
> 8 very small white turnips
> 2 cups green beans
> 18 very small white onions
> 2 cups fresh peas or 2 packages frozen peas, thawed

Heat the oven to 325° F.

Remove as much fat as possible from the lamb shoulder and trim off the gristle. Cut into 2-inch serving pieces—the butcher will do this for you if you ask him politely. Heat 3 Tbsp. of the olive oil in a heavy skillet and brown the pieces of lamb thoroughly on all sides. Add more oil as it is needed. The surface of the pan should be little more than well-oiled; if you use too much the meat will stew and the process will become very tedious.

Transfer the meat to a heavy 6-quart casserole with a lid. Sprinkle with the sugar and put the casserole over high heat for 7 or 8 minutes, stirring all the while with a wooden spoon. Add 1 Tbsp. coarse salt and ½ tsp. freshly ground black pepper. Sprinkle with the flour and cook for 5 minutes longer. Add the chopped tomatoes, crushed garlic, thyme, bay leaf and the stock or consommé. Cover and cook in the oven for 1 hour. Test for doneness—the meat should be firm but almost tender enough to serve. Remove the meat to a clean pan and strain the sauce. Cool and remove the fat, if any. Reheat the sauce and pour it over the meat.

Bring 2 quarts of water to which you have added 2 Tbsp. salt to a boil.

Cook the carrots and turnips in the boiling salted water until almost done—they must remain firm. Using the same water, cook the green beans and the white onions for 4 minutes. Add all the vegetables, including the raw peas, to the meat in its sauce and reheat in a temperate, 325° oven for approximately half an hour, or until hot enough to serve.

New Potatoes in Mint Vinaigrette

    24 new potatoes of uniform size
    2   quarts water
    2   Tbsp. salt
    2   sprays or large sprigs mint
    1   mixing vinaigrette dressing (page 23) to which
        8–10 crushed mint leaves have been added
    ¼   cup parsley sprigs, chopped

Peel the potatoes and cook them in the salted water with a spray or 2 of mint until tender, being careful not to overcook. They should look firm but be easily pierced with a wooden toothpick. Drain thoroughly and allow them to dry for 5 minutes.

Pour the dressing over the potatoes while they are still warm and mix thoroughly. Arrange them in their serving bowl or platter and allow them to cool to room temperature. Sprinkle the chopped parsley over the dish before serving.

Raspberry Sorbet

Syrup:

    1   cup water
    3   cups sugar

    2   cups raspberry purée—4 cups fresh raspberries or
        2 10-oz. packages of frozen berries will be needed
    2   Tbsp. fresh lemon juice
    2   egg whites
    Electric ice-cream maker

In a small enamel-coated or stainless steel pan, dissolve the sugar in the water over low heat. When it is completely dissolved turn up the heat and boil rapidly for 5 minutes exactly (or bring to a temperature of 216° F. on a candy thermometer). Remove from the heat and cool.

Rub the fresh raspberries through a fine wire sieve or strainer—there should be no seeds in the purée. If you must use frozen fruit, defrost first and then drain and force through a sieve or strainer. (I find a large metal spoon the best forcer.) Add the lemon juice and mix with the cooled syrup.

Pour this mixture into the canister of an electric ice-cream maker, then pack the container with crushed ice and coarse salt in the proportion of 3 to 1-3 cups of ice with 1 cup of salt poured on top. Continue till the container is almost full, but do not allow the ice and salt to come above the top of the canister. Freeze for 20 minutes, then stop the motor and open the canister. The mixture should be of the consistency of wet snow. If it is too soft and watery, continue freezing for another 5 minutes. Beat the egg whites and fold into the slush in the canister: simply remove the dasher and stir very gently with a long-handled spoon. If the ice has been reduced by too much, pack the canister with more ice and salt. Put the lid back on and freeze for a further 20 minutes. By now the ice should be well formed, pliable but not solid.

Store in the freezer compartment of your refrigerator for at least an hour before using.

A Small Chocolate Cake

> 4 oz. unsweetened chocolate
> 3 oz. (¾ stick) butter, allowed to soften almost to
>   room temperature
> 2 Tbsp. flour
> ½ cup sugar
> 3 eggs, separated

Frosting:

½ cup sweet chocolate pieces
1 Tbsp. sugar
2 Tbsp. water or less
1 oz. softened butter
1 Tbsp. dark rum

Heat the oven to 350° F.

To make the cake, melt the chocolate over hot, not boiling water. Mix with the softened butter, flour, sugar and well-beaten egg yolks. Fold in the stiffly beaten egg whites. Spoon into a lightly buttered and sugared 6-inch round cake pan or loaf tin, and bake in the preheated 350° oven for 35 minutes. The cake will have a thin crust on top and will seem, if tested, to be too soft or insufficiently cooked, but this is the way it should be. It gets firmer as it cools. When cool, turn it out onto a cake rack.

For the frosting, melt the chocolate with the sugar and water over hot water. When the chocolate has melted, stir until it's very smooth, then stir in the butter and the dark rum. Allow to cool, then cover the sides and top of the cake.

As stated in the introductory notes, this cake may be baked and frozen as much as a week beforehand so long as you frost it after it's thawed but should be allowed to thaw overnight in the refrigerator. Or it may be made a day ahead and refrigerated; but in either case it should be taken out of the refrigerator 2 or 3 hours before you serve it.

❧ AUTUMN ❧

Autumn is forever associated in my memory with the smell of burning leaves and of chrysanthemums, with nuts and apples, and the reds, browns and golds of the harvest. Even now the earthy-metallic smell of chrysanthemums, if I come across them at the height of the summer, will make me feel suddenly catapulted into fall, for in my younger days chrysanthemums were brought into the house only after the first frost. It was the time of taking in the last of summer's food, bottling and canning the last fruits and vegetables, drying herbs, making pickles.

The first nip in the air is likely to reawaken our appetites, as if to prompt us to take in nourishment in preparation for a long winter. New menus suggest themselves. We are inclined again toward richer soups, heartier preparations of beef and lamb and seafood, baked custards or puddings and fall fruits, apples, pears and grapes. And the wealth of the harvest is celebrated of course at Thanksgiving with a traditional menu embracing an array of foods that might support us for a month, floating us along nicely into the year-end holidays.

AUTUMN LUNCHEON

Celery Rémoulade
Panaquette de Saumon Fumé
Iced Ginger Parfait

Serves 6 to 8

This luncheon for an autumn day is elegant, yet in fact simple to prepare. With the exception of making the crêpes for the panaquette, which must be done at least a day ahead, it may all be prepared in the morning.

Sauce Rémoulade is based on mayonnaise, either of your own making or a good commercial brand, its flavor sharpened with lemon juice to suit your palate. It may be prepared well ahead of time and refrigerated, then mixed with the celery about twenty minutes before lunch and served as a first course.

The panaquette is a very rich, sophisticated dish which is easy to make and may be served either for a special luncheon or as a first course for an otherwise light and sparing dinner. As I suggested in the spring menu for the Crêpes de Volaille, it seems to me always a good idea to make a great many crêpes once you set out to do them. Most refrigerators will yield enough at any time to make a sweet or savory filling, and, again, the crêpes may be frozen with complete confidence.

The smoked salmon should be of the finest quality—the Scotch is the best, in my opinion, with Nova Scotia a close runner-up. But as it will eventually be chopped before being mixed with hollandaise and rolled up in the crêpes, it need not be bought sliced paper thin, as it would be for serving with brown bread and butter. Often the storekeeper will let you have small pieces at a very much reduced price.

The recipe for the hollandaise is anxiety-proof. Do not attempt to serve it hot—hollandaise is always served lukewarm. Remember that it is not heat, but sudden heat that causes the sauce to curdle; and it is not cooking, but overcooking that scrambles the egg yolks. The beaten egg yolks are gently heated before the hot melted butter is added—and if the sauce is not thick enough and needs extra heat, be careful not to overdo it.

Use seasonings with discretion—the lemon juice is there only to accentuate the flavor of the fresh eggs and butter. A useful guide to its proportions is that one egg yolk will absorb approximately four ounces of butter.

Make the hollandaise in the morning, dribble a little melted butter over the surface to prevent a skin from forming and cover the bowl with plastic wrap. Fill the crêpes as early in the day as you wish and brush them with melted butter, but don't refrigerate them. And don't be sidetracked into taking short cuts that will get you nowhere; specifically, do not try to mask the crêpes with hollandaise and then heat the dish in the oven, as it won't work.

Ginger, I think, is an acquired taste, but once on to it you are hooked forever. Served in a parfait about twenty minutes out of the freezer it makes a wonderfully tart and satisfying dessert. It may be made long in advance, as it freezes beautifully and is in fact a very useful confection to have on hand in your freezer.

Celery Rémoulade

    10 stalks very fresh and crisp celery
    Lettuce leaves

Rémoulade Sauce:

    2 cups mayonnaise—better if homemade
    2 Tbsp. finely chopped cucumber pickle
    2 Tbsp. drained, finely chopped capers
    2 tsp. imported French mustard
    1 Tbsp. finely chopped parsley
    1 tsp. chopped tarragon
    1 tsp. chopped chervil
    1 tsp. anchovy paste
    Lemon juice (optional)

Combine all the ingredients for the sauce and mix well. Add the lemon juice if you think the sauce is not sharp enough.

Wash the celery and remove any tough outer fibers with a vegetable scraper. Slice very thinly on the bias to get elongated strips. If it's not to be used right away, store it in a plastic bag until needed. Mix with the dressing about 20 to 30 minutes before serving. Serve each portion on a lettuce leaf.

Panaquette de Saumon Fumé

    1 recipe crêpes (see page 64)
    Hollandaise Sauce
    ½ lb. smoked salmon
    2-3 Tbsp. chopped parsley

Hollandaise Sauce:

    6-7 oz. or 10-12 Tbsp. butter
    3 egg yolks
    Salt and pepper
    Lemon juice

Make the crêpes according to the instructions on page 64.

To make the hollandaise, mix the egg yolks thoroughly in a warmed bowl with a whisk or electric beater, going very slowly. Do not beat to a froth.

Melt the butter in a heavy saucepan. When it's foaming, pour it onto the egg yolks in a thin stream while beating with a whisk or beater. If the yolks are warm and the butter hot enough you should now have hollandaise. If not, stand the bowl in a larger pan of hot water over gentle heat and whisk until thickened, being careful not to overheat. Season with salt, pepper and lemon juice.

Heat the oven to 350° F.

Chop the smoked salmon coarsely and mix it with ½ cup of the hollandaise.

Fill 2 crêpes for each person you are serving, and several extra if you wish, with approximately 1 Tbsp. of the smoked salmon and hollandaise mixture, turning in the sides and rolling the crêpe up neatly. Butter a shallow, ovenproof dish and arrange the filled crêpes in it. Heat in the oven for 20 minutes. Then spread the crêpes generously with hollandaise and glaze under the broiler until the sauce bubbles. Sprinkle with chopped parsley before serving.

Iced Ginger Parfait

> ¾ cup sugar
> ⅓ cup water
> 4 egg yolks
> Salt
> 2 cups heavy cream
> 2 tsp. ground ginger
> 4 Tbsp. lemon juice
> 4 oz. crystallized ginger, finely chopped

Cook the sugar and water in a heavy saucepan until the syrup spins a thread (230° on a candy thermometer). Beat the egg yolks and a dash of salt thoroughly, then beat the hot syrup into the egg yolks in a thin stream and continue beating until cool.

Beat together the heavy cream, ground ginger and lemon juice until the cream holds definite peaks. Fold in the cooled yolk mixture along with the crystallized ginger. This will make 12 servings if you spoon it into ⅓-cup ramekins, or spoon it into a 1-quart soufflé dish. Freeze until firm, and remove from the freezer about 20 minutes before serving.

AUTUMN DINNER

Indian River Soup
Plymouth Leg of Lamb
Poires Dijonnaises
Zucchini and Yellow Squash
Crystallized Grapes

Serves 6 to 8

The autumn dinner is all a well-planned menu should be in its contrast in color, flavor and texture. The meal is a delight first to the eye and then to the palate.

The tomato soup flavored with orange is one of my favorites, and I like to emphasize its rich color by serving it in blue and white Chinese rice grain bowls. I like it cold as well as hot, and should there be any left over (which is most unlikely) I will gladly drink it first thing in the morning in place of fruit juice. It is easy to prepare and kind to those who are avoiding weight-making foods.

The Plymouth Leg of Lamb is named for the brand of gin, one of Britain's oldest gins and the one most favored in the Royal Navy's Ward Room. It is prepared with juniper berries soaked in gin, which allay the strong flavor of older lamb. I can safely say that this dish is not an acquired taste—the first time I served it, it was received with great acclaim.

Buy a leg of lamb weighing not more than five pounds, and ask your butcher to bone it. He will probably be obliging and more than willing to perform these chores if you show an intelligent interest in his skill. A casually dropped hint as to how you intend to prepare the lamb will invariably whet his appetites. Juniper berries are not difficult to come by—they can be found in stores that carry a selection of spices and sometimes in drugstores.

Forty-five to fifty minutes is sufficient cooking time to produce medium-rare or pink meat, which is the way I prefer it. Nothing is more unappetizing than overcooked lamb that has a battleship gray look to it. Allow the lamb to rest for ten or fifteen minutes after it is taken out of the oven, as you should many roasted meats. This allows the juices to settle so that they will not be lost as soon as the knife is plunged into the leg. Carve thin slices and ignore the berries that give the inside of the meat the appearance of the inside of a cut papaya with its tightly packed seeds. One is not expected to eat the berries, but it does no harm to crunch one or two to fully appreciate the unusual flavor.

The cooking method for the zucchini and yellow squash is an abbreviated stir-fry; if you are fortunate enough to own a wok, it is a stir-fry proper. No water is needed and the amount of fat required minimal. Use fat sparingly until the salt has been added, at which point the juices will flow and produce sufficient moisture to prevent sticking and burning. If you are avoiding butter you may use vegetable oil. This method may be applied to other vegetables as well.

Pears are at their best at this time of year and the Anjou is my favorite, with Comice a close second. Choose firm unblemished fruit with the stems intact. If the pear is overripe, it will cook before it has had time to absorb the flavors of the syrup. Remember always to allow poached fruit to cool in its syrup before chilling, then drain as it comes out of the refrigerator before spooning the sauce over it. The sauce originated in the area of Dijon. The marriage of black currants and raspberries is a happy and unusual one and the simple sauce might well be put to other uses.

Indian River Soup

> 1-lb. can plum tomatoes with basil
> 1 carrot, shredded
> ½ of one medium onion, chopped
> 1 bay leaf
> Rind of one lemon
> 6 peppercorns
> 3 cups clear beef or chicken consommé
> 2 Tbsp. sugar
> ½ cup dry white vermouth
> Salt and freshly ground pepper (preferably white)
> Rind of one orange
> Juice of one orange
> 2 Tbsp. finely chopped parsley

In a heavy 2-quart pan bring to a boil then simmer very gently for 8 minutes the tomatoes, the carrot, the onion, bay leaf, lemon rind and peppercorns. Strain carefully into a mixing bowl. Rinse the pot and return the tomato liquid to the clean pot, then add the beef or chicken consommé. Put over moderate heat and add the sugar and vermouth. Continue heating almost to the boiling point, then season with salt and freshly ground pepper. (In this case I prefer white pepper, and proceed cautiously as the soup can suddenly become very hot.)

Meanwhile, peel the orange very carefully with a vegetable peeler, avoiding the white pith, then cut the peel into very thin strips half an inch long. Put the peel aside to be used as a garnish and squeeze the orange, adding the juice to the soup. Ladle the soup into bowls or soup plates and sprinkle with finely chopped parsley and the orange rind. This soup may also be served cold in case the weather is unusually warm.

Plymouth Leg of Lamb

> 1 leg of lamb weighing not more than 5 lbs., boned
> 1 cup gin
> ½ cup juniper berries
> Coarse salt and freshly ground black pepper
> 4–6 oz. unsalted butter

Soak the juniper berries overnight in half a cup of the gin, sealing the glass to prevent evaporation. In the morning before the lamb is to be cooked, flatten it out and season the cut side very generously with coarse salt, freshly ground black pepper, and half the butter. Spread the juniper berries over the seasoned lamb, roll it up and sew the leg together with a large needle and string, then refrigerate until needed.

Heat the oven to 450° F.

Take the leg of lamb out of the refrigerator and spread the rest of the butter over it. Season it again with salt and pepper. Put it on a rack in a roasting pan and cook for 45 to 50 minutes, basting it with its juices from time to time.

Once out of the oven, let it rest for 10 to 15 minutes on a heated platter, then heat the other half-cup of the gin, pour it over the lamb and set it alight. When the flames die down, carve in thin slices.

Zucchini and Yellow Squash

> 4 small yellow squash
> 3 small zucchini
> 2 Tbsp. red pimiento
> ¼ cup finely chopped parsley
> 1 lemon
> 3 Tbsp. butter
> 2 Tbsp. oil, vegetable or olive
> Salt and freshly ground black pepper
> 1 Tbsp. sugar

Wash but do not peel the squash and zucchini and cut a thin slice from each end. Slice in half lengthwise and then slice each half in half again. Cut the slices into ½-inch square dice. Chop the pimiento. Chop the parsley and grate and squeeze the lemon.

Melt 2 Tbsp. of the butter in a heavy 3–4-quart pan or skillet. Add 1 Tbsp. of oil, and, when it is really hot, the zucchini and squash. Mix well to coat each piece of the vegetable with oil and butter. Cook over gentle heat for 3 to 4 minutes. Add 1 tsp. salt and continue cooking for 2 to 3 minutes with the lid on the pan or skillet. Take off the lid and if the vegetables look very dry, add the remainder of the butter and oil. (The addition of the salt usually brings out moisture so that further fats are not needed.)

Add the juice of half the lemon and cook 2 minutes longer. Remember to test the vegetables from time to time. (The timing given here is only a guide—vegetables vary in age and freshness and the cooking time varies accordingly. The zucchini and squash should hold their shape and be served crisp instead of in a mush.) Add the lemon rind to the pan, mix thoroughly and add the sugar. Stir in the chopped pimiento and parsley. Season with freshly ground black pepper and add more salt if you think it's necessary. This dish may be prepared ahead of time if you are careful to undercook it. Heat gently when needed.

Poires Dijonnaises

    6-to-8 pears, Anjou or Comice (not too ripe)
    1 12-ounce packet frozen raspberries, thawed and drained
    ½ cup black currant jam

Poaching Syrup:

    2 quarts water
    3 cups sugar
    4 sticks cinnamon
    8 whole cloves
    1 lemon, cut in quarters

To make the syrup, dissolve the sugar in the water in a large pan with a lid. Add the cinnamon sticks, cloves and lemon quarters. Simmer for half an hour with the lid on.

Peel the pears and cut a thin slice from the bottom of each so that they will stand upright. Add them to the syrup and simmer gently until they are soft when pierced with a toothpick—be careful not to overcook them. Allow them to cool in the syrup.

Rub both the raspberries and the black currant jam through a fine strainer and mix thoroughly for the sauce.

Arrange the pears in a serving dish and spoon some of the sauce over them—the rest should be passed separately.

Crystallized Grapes

> 1 small bunch of near-perfect seedless green grapes
> 1 cup sugar
> ¼ cup hot water
> Baking sheet, lightly oiled

Divide the bunch of grapes into very much smaller bunches—clusters of 3 or 4 are perfect—and discard any damaged grapes, since their juices will leak through the sugar coating. Do not wash them.

Pour the hot water over the sugar in a small pan and stir until it's dissolved. Put the pan on the highest heat the stove is capable of and boil for 8 to 10 minutes or until the temperature on a candy thermometer reaches 280°. If you don't have a thermometer heat until the liquid forms a thin, hard thread when a metal spoon is dipped into it and then lifted.

Now hold a small cluster of grapes by its stem, dip it into the syrup, swirl it around to coat each one thoroughly and hold it up to allow the excess to drip off. Hold it in your hand for a few seconds to dry before putting it on the very lightly oiled baking sheet.

To serve the grapes, arrange them on a suitable dish and pass them after dessert in place of petit fours.

AUTUMN BUFFET

Seafood Fricassee   *Sirloin of Beef in Casserole*

Saffron Rice   *Salad Espagnole*

Pita

Caramel Lottie   *Baked Stuffed Apples*

Apricot Cream

Serves 12 to 14

This is a rather unexpected collection of substantial and appealing dishes which you will find make up a wonderful menu for a moderate-sized supper party. The dishes are all quite easy and straightforward in their preparation and will serve you well individually as the central ingredients of much more limited gatherings.

Seafood is unfailingly popular and this fricassee is made entirely from readily available ingredients. It may be varied according to your whim or what looks best at the fish counter: you may, for example, want to add sole, mussels or squid to the lobster, crab, shrimp and scallops the recipe calls for. The only point to remember is that the various ingredients must be suitably prepared and added at the right time. The relatively tough squid, for example, once the center is removed and it has been cut up into small pieces, would need to be sautéed for two or three minutes before adding the shrimp and the more delicate seafoods. Sole or mussels would be the last ingredient to go into the sauté, requiring only a minute's cooking before the addition of the liquids.

The fricassee can be made no earlier than the morning of the party, and must be allowed to cool thoroughly before it's refrigerated. However, the beef casserole, like most dishes of its kind, is much better made the day before. This allows ample time for the various flavors to amalgamate, and makes the skimming of any congealed fat from the surface a very easy matter. It's a marvelously rich dish using a good cut of meat (I would advise you to go to a butcher for the two-inch-thick sirloin) and requiring no other flavoring than the bouillon, mushrooms and Madeira with which it's prepared. Once the cooking time is up, you need do nothing more than lift the meat onto one serving dish and pour its sauce into another.

The saffron rice, which we have encountered as a part of the paella, goes beautifully with both the seafood and the beef. It must be made not from the adulterated product sold as saffron powder, but from the real saffron filaments: the dried stamens of the autumn crocus. These filaments look like very thin orange threads, and because of their pungency and their high cost (approximately 90,000 flowers are needed for one pound of stamens) they are used very sparingly. One-quarter of a teaspoon of saffron is sufficient to flavor and color rice for four people.

Pita, the Middle Eastern bread, was discussed in the Sunday Brunch menu—again, buy the whole wheat variety if you can find it. Once prepared as the recipe specifies (separated in two, then quartered, buttered and toasted), it may be successfully frozen and reheated as wanted.

The Salad Espagnole has the useful virtue of standing up well to the passing of time and will continue to look fresh through a lengthy appearance on your buffet table. It may be made in the morning so long as the dressing is not added until shortly before it is served.

Both the caramel custard and the baked apples may be made a day in advance and taken out of the refrigerator an hour or so before the meal to let them warm up to room temperature. And the apricot cream, which goes very well with either dessert, may be prepared an hour before dinner is served.

Caramel Lottie is the standard caramel custard, but with caramel added to the custard itself. This is because I find that in the conventional preparation, most of the caramel used to line the dish remains there and little rubs off on the dessert. The caramel flavor is delicious, and its strength may be determined by the length of its cooking time—the longer the caramel syrup is cooked, the darker and more bitter it becomes. My preference is a dark amber color.

Baked apples are everyday fare but when they are stuffed with a fruit mixture such as nesselrode they can take their place on any menu no matter how sophisticated. Nesselrode, like mincemeat, may be purchased in a jar in most supermarkets, and I add brown sugar, raisins and the juice and grated rind of a lemon to give it an extra zing.

Seafood Fricassee

> ½ lb. fresh shrimp, small
> ½ lb. fresh frozen lobster
> ½ lb. fresh frozen crabmeat
> ½ lb. bay scallops
> 2 oz. (½ stick) butter
> ½ cup tomato purée
> ½ cup dry white vermouth
> ½ lb. mushrooms, sliced thin
> 2 Tbsp. cornstarch
> ½ cup heavy cream
> Salt and freshly ground black pepper
> ½ cup parsley sprigs, chopped

Peel, devein and wash the shrimp and cut them in half lengthwise. Thaw and drain the lobster and crabmeat and rinse under cold running water. Rinse the scallops.

Melt the butter in a heavy pan or skillet. Add the shrimp and cook, turning with a spoon, for 3 to 4 minutes. Add the scallops and cook for 3 minutes longer. Stir in the tomato purée and add the vermouth. Add the lobster, mushrooms and crabmeat and cook 2 minutes longer.

Moisten the cornstarch with a little water to make a smooth paste, mix with the heavy cream and stir into the seafood mixture. Season with salt and pepper to taste and heat until thickened. Serve sprinkled with chopped parsley.

Sirloin of Beef in Casserole

> 6 lbs. sirloin in 2 pieces, each about 2 inches thick
> ½ lb. mushrooms
> ½ cup beef bouillon
> ½ cup dry Madeira
> 2 Tbsp. olive oil
> ¼ cup flour
> 2 tsp. salt
> ½ tsp. black pepper

Heat the oven to 400° F.

Trim most of the fat from the meat. Wipe the mushrooms with a damp cloth and slice them very thin. Heat the bouillon and Madeira together in a small saucepan.

Heat the oil in a heavy skillet. Dust the sirloin generously with flour, then brown both pieces thoroughly on all sides. Transfer the meat to a casserole with a lid, and add the mushrooms. (If you don't own a casserole large enough to hold both pieces of meat side by side, place one above the other with the mushrooms in between.) Add approximately 2 tsp. salt and ½ tsp. pepper. Pour the bouillon and Madeira over the meat, cover and cook for 35 minutes.

If you have made this dish ahead of time, allow it to cool and then refrigerate, skimming off any fat after it has set. Reheat in a 325° oven for about half an hour or until heated through, then remove the meat to a serving dish and pour the sauce into a sauceboat or tureen. Carve the meat in thin strips and allow your guests to help themselves to sauce.

Saffron Rice

> 3 cups long-grain rice
> ½ tsp. saffron
> ¼ cup hot water

Cook the rice in 3 to 4 quarts of boiling salted water (using about 1½ Tbsp. of salt per quart of water). Cook al dente, beginning to test grains with your teeth 12 minutes after the water has returned to a boil.

Meanwhile, dissolve the saffron in the ¼ cup hot water, allow it to soak for about 15 minutes, then strain the bright orange infused liquid into the rice about halfway through its estimated cooking time.

Salad Espagnole

> 2 Tbsp. salt
> 1 lb. fresh green beans
> 4 ripe tomatoes

1 4-oz. jar of pimiento
1 red onion
1 lb. firm white mushrooms
1 mixing vinaigrette dressing (page 23)
1 cup parsley sprigs, chopped coarsely

Fill a heavy pan holding at least 2 quarts with water, add 2 Tbsp. salt and bring it to a boil. Top and tail the beans and put them in the pot. When the water comes to a boil again, cook for 4 minutes or until al dente.

After the beans have come out, drop the tomatoes into the same boiling water, count to ten, lift them out and remove the skins. Slice and, if they are large, cut each slice in half. Drain and dice the pimiento. Slice the red onion very thinly. Wipe the mushrooms with a damp cloth, cut off the stems flush with the caps and slice them very thinly.

Put all the vegetables in a salad bowl and refrigerate until just before serving (this preparation may be done in the morning, if you like, and the dressing mixed but not refrigerated). Then mix the dressing into the salad with ¾ of the chopped parsley, scattering the remainder over the salad just before you bring it to the table.

Pita

2 packages or 5 to 6 pita
Butter

Split each pita into its top and bottom rounds, prying the loosely joined halves apart with a bread knife. Spread each half generously with butter, then cut each into quarters and toast briefly under the broiler until light brown. (Prepared this way, the pita keeps well when frozen.) Serve piled high in a breadbasket.

Caramel Lottie

2 cups sugar
1 cup hot water
3 cups milk
8 whole eggs

8 egg yolks
½ cup sugar
2 one-quart soufflé dishes

Heat the oven to 375° F.

Put the 2 cups of sugar in a heavy pan (preferably one that you do not treasure) and add ½ cup of the hot water. Stir till the sugar is dissolved, then put it on the stove over very high heat and cook without stirring until the syrup is dark amber in color. Once the syrup begins to change color it goes very quickly and continues to darken after the pan has been taken off the range.

Taking great care and wearing a glove on the hand that holds the pan, pour the other half cup of hot water into the syrup pan. The boiling syrup often spatters, but if the half-cup of water is heated to boiling, the spattering will be minimized. Stir the mixture until it's smooth and all the caramel has dissolved.

Meanwhile, heat the 3 cups of milk very gently. The temperature should be little more than blood-heat, or, as some chefs describe it, tongue temperature. To check for this temperature, leave a metal spoon in the pan of milk and every so often test a spoonful with your tongue. Then stir the caramel into the warm milk, mixing well.

Break the 8 whole eggs into a large bowl. Add the 8 egg yolks to the bowl, and freeze their whites for another day. Beat the eggs and yolks until light in color, adding the ½ cup of sugar gradually. Continue beating for a minute or two. Pour on the warm caramel-flavored milk and mix thoroughly. Strain this mixture into the soufflé dishes and stand the dishes in a roasting pan, adding enough hot water to reach ¾ of the way up the sides. Cover with double thickness of brown paper. Cook in the oven for 45 minutes. When taken out of the oven, the center will look thin and liquid—however, the custard will continue to cook a little longer while it cools. Chill thoroughly before turning out on serving dish. I'd suggest putting one custard at a time out on the serving table.

Baked Stuffed Apples

>   2 cups dry cake crumbs, preferably from a pound cake
>   8 Granny Smith or Greening apples
>   6 Tbsp. butter, softened
>   Half of 1 10-oz. jar of nesselrode
>   ¼ cup brown sugar
>   1½ oz. (2 Tbsp.) seedless raisins
>   Rind of 1 lemon, grated
>   Juice of 1 lemon

Heat the oven to 375° F.

To prepare the cake crumbs, chop up about a half a good commercial or bakery-bought pound cake, spread the pieces on a baking sheet, and put them in a 275°–300° oven for however long they need to dry out, then crush them with a rolling pin between sheets of waxed paper to make crumbs.

Peel and core the apples. Remove the stalk and core, enlarging the hole to make room for the filling, but be careful not to pierce the bottom so that the filling won't leak out. Using 4 Tbsp. of the softened butter, coat each apple thoroughly, then roll it in the cake crumbs and place on a buttered baking sheet with raised edges.

Mix the nesselrode with the brown sugar, raisins, grated rind and juice of the lemon. Pack the apples with this mixture and put a small piece of butter on the top of each. Pour a little water into the pan—just enough to keep the bottoms from burning—before putting it in the oven.

Bake for 45 minutes or until tender. Test by putting a skewer or heavy toothpick into the side of each apple—cooking time will differ for each depending on its ripeness. If there is any syrup or juice in the bottom of the pan, spoon it over the apples while they are still hot, then allow them to cool before refrigerating or serving. They are best eaten at room temperature.

Apricot Cream

>   1 cup heavy cream, well chilled
>   ½ cup apricot jam or purée, the tarter the better

If you're using jam, put it through a fine strainer, then add it or the purée to the cream and chill in the freezing compartment of your refrigerator for 15 minutes before beating. Beat till the cream mixture holds peaks. This may be done an hour or so before serving and the whipped apricot cream kept in the refrigerator until it's put out on the table.

THANKSGIVING DINNER

Oyster Bisque   *Corn Sticks*
Half-Boned Turkey   *Giblet Sauce*
Carrots   *Turnips*   *Green Beans*
Cranberry Chutney   *Potato Purée*
Pumpkin Mousse
Fruits   *Nuts*

Serves 12

The celebration of a bountiful harvest is by no means an exclusively American holiday: a day appointed to a harvest thanksgiving was customary throughout Europe centuries before the Pilgrims crossed the ocean to the New World. We know that pre-Christian Europeans sacrificed livestock and offered the produce of their lands to their gods at harvest time. Christianity absorbed a part of these ancient rites, as in the rural districts of most of Europe farmers celebrated a day of thanksgiving in their churches. Even in recent times parishioners would bring some offering of their crops to decorate the church—perhaps a few choice apples, bunches of asters, sheaves of corn or wheat, and the pumpkins and vegetable marrows so dear to the English gardener and so large they almost overwhelmed the altar.

The extent of what has become the traditional Thanksgiving feast in the United States came as a surprise to me: I simply could not envisage the Pilgrims eating their way through most of the past season's crop at one sitting. What surely must have started as a modest occasion, on which the Pilgrims celebrated their survival as well as the probably customary offering of thanks for the harvest, has become a notable American holiday. For me, the charm of this occasion is that Americans, no matter where they live, feel drawn to their families at this time, and think nothing of traveling the length or breadth of the continent to reach them. Peace and calm prevail, and the spirit of good will is very like that of Christmas in my native land.

The first Thanksgiving Day I spent in America was in 1946, when I was persuaded to put off sailing for England in order to have dinner with some people I had never met who lived in an 18th-century Connecticut farmhouse. I shall never forget the welcome these two people who were then strangers gave me and their other guests, putting us all to work helping to decorate the house or to prepare dinner. On the table were two perfect red cabbages arranged in old porcelain bedpans and with candles in tall silver candelabra. And the meal remains one of the best Thanksgiving menus I have ever shared.

The dinner began with soup, good and substantial without being too heavy—I think an oyster bisque. With it there was hot cornbread about as thick as two fingers, my first encounter with this delicacy. The turkey with its chestnut stuffing followed, as well as vegetables and puréed potatoes and a sauce made from the turkey giblets and pan juices thickened naturally by slow reduction to the right consistency. I was already acquainted with pumpkin pie through some American friends living in England, or I would have been surprised that such a use should be made of the humble pumpkin. The pie was followed by great dishes of fresh fruit and nuts, and if I remember rightly I was moved to make a speech in gratitude for the war's being over and in praise of living on this wonderful earth in peace—but that was a long time ago, and it didn't seem possible to us then that there could be another war.

My Thanksgiving dinner is very like that one of twenty-seven years ago. The oyster soup can be prepared ahead of time—in fact, oysters may be bought already shucked. The turkey will be half boned for easier carving; and if you are serving a very large number of people, cook two turkeys rather than a single very large bird—they will taste better. All the work of stuffing and preparing the turkey for roasting may be done the evening before, refrigerating the oven-ready bird until cooking time. The vegetables may be prepared and left in cold water until Thanksgiving afternoon. Make the pumpkin mousse the day before and refrigerate it. Decorate your table with bowls of fresh fruit and nuts, to be eaten after dessert with, if you like, small glasses of port.

This is a rich meal by my standards, but it includes all that is expected on this occasion, and in comparison with many Thanksgiving dinners that have been served to me is downright frugal. Don't allow too much time before dinner for drinking, and serve a Pinot Noir which will be light enough to keep at bay that overloaded feeling that usually accompanies this festive meal. Serve small portions so that your guests may eat sparingly if they choose and you will be remembered as having served a traditional Thanksgiving dinner which left your guests with light hearts and even lighter stomachs.

Oyster Bisque

> 4 Tbsp. butter
> 2 Tbsp. finely chopped shallots or scallions (white part only)
> 4 pints oysters with their liquid
> 4 cups half-and-half or light cream
> Salt, grated nutmeg and white pepper for seasoning
> 1 cup parsley sprigs, finely chopped

Melt the butter in a heavy pan and add the finely chopped shallots or scallions. Cook very gently until they are transparent, being most careful not to allow them to become brown.

Stand the pan in a larger one of hot water over medium heat. Add the oysters and their liquid. Stir carefully until the oysters curl at the edge. Heat the half-and-half to just below boiling point and stir it into the oysters. Season to taste with grated nutmeg, salt and white pepper. Heat gently and on no account allow the soup to boil. Stir in the chopped parsley just before serving.

Serve with the hot corn sticks.

Corn Sticks

> 1 cup sifted all-purpose flour
> 2½ tsp. double-acting baking powder
> 1 Tbsp. sugar
> ¾ tsp. salt
> 1½ cups yellow corn meal
> 1 large egg
> ¾ cup milk
> 3 Tbsp. melted butter
> 2 corn-stick baking tins to hold about 30 sticks—butter the tins lightly and heat them in the oven

Heat the oven to 425° F.

Combine all the dry ingredients in a bowl. In a second bowl, beat the egg with the milk and melted butter. Stir the liquid into the dry ingredients. Spoon the batter into the buttered corn-stick pans, but do not fill them quite to the top. Bake for 20 to 25 minutes.

Serve the corn sticks warm, cradled in a white napkin in a bread basket.

Half-Boned Turkey

> 1 fresh turkey, approximately 12 lbs., cleaned but not trussed
> 3 tsp. coarse salt
> ½ tsp. freshly ground black pepper
> 2 tsp. lemon juice
> ¼ lb. (1 stick) unsalted butter, softened
> 1 small can truffles, or 1 fresh truffle cut in very thin slices
> 4 chicken breasts (from 2 chickens), boned and skinned
> ¼ cup flour

Stock for the Giblet Sauce:

> Giblets and bones of turkey
> Bones from chicken breasts
> ½ cup onion, coarsely chopped
> 2 stalks celery
> 1 carrot, chopped
> 1 bay leaf
> 1 Tbsp. salt
> 6 peppercorns
> Water to cover

Stuffing:

> 2 lbs. lean pork, ground
> 1 lb. stewing veal, ground
> 5 cups dried chestnuts, soaked in water overnight, then cooked until tender and coarsely chopped
> 2 cups fresh whole-wheat bread crumbs
> 1 cup finely chopped green celery tops
> 1 tsp. dried thyme
> 2 Tbsp. salt

Dry the outside of the turkey and remove the giblets, which are usually tucked inside. Turn it on its back and with a sharp knife, preferably one made for boning, make a cut through the skin from tail to neck following the line of the breast bone. Carefully ease the skin away from the breast, cutting the thin membrane attaching it when necessary. Continue until all the skin has been freed and there are 2 flaps, one on each side.

Holding the knife at an angle with the sharp edge toward the bone, ease the breast on either side away from the bone, using your fingers when necessary. When the breast meat from tail to back has been released you will find a V-shaped bone connected to the wing joint by a ball and socket joint. With the blade of the knife ease the ball from the socket. Repeat on the other side and remove each half of the breast intact. Cut out the wish bone. The rib cage is now visible and if you examine it carefully you will see that it is made up of two sets of ribs, one pointing upwards and the other down. They don't quite meet. Cut the membrane between the upper and lower sets and the top half of the rib cage will come away in one piece. You are now left with a boat shape and 2 skin flaps.

Put all the stock ingredients in a heavy 3- to 4-quart pan and cover with cold water. Bring to a boil and reduce the heat so that it simmers gently. Simmer while preparing the stuffing.

In a large mixing bowl combine all the ingredients for the stuffing and mix thoroughly. Sprinkle the inside of the topless turkey with salt and pepper and lemon juice and spread generously with softened butter. Pile the stuffing in the boat-shaped cavity and mold to a natural form. Slice the half chicken breasts in half; you will now have 8 pieces. Slice the turkey breasts in half; you will have 4 pieces. Lay the chicken breasts on the mounded stuffing. Brush with softened butter and lay the thinly sliced truffles on top. Then cover the chicken breasts with the turkey breasts and season once more with salt and pepper. Bring the skin flaps up to cover the replaced breast meat and arrange them so that they meet where the breast bone should be. With an upholsterer's or larding needle and fine string sew the flaps together using long stitches and sew up the openings at each end of the bird. Push both drumsticks well forward and run a long broiling skewer through the drumstick and on through the carcass so that it emerges through the drumstick on the other side. Put a second long broiling skewer through the second wing joint, through the carcass and out through the wing joint on the other side of the bird. Tie a piece of string to the end of one skewer and loop it round the end of the other on the same side of the bird. Pull to bring the skewers together, then repeat on the other side. This makes a very neat and compact bird now ready for the oven.

Heat the oven to 350° F.

Brush the entire surface of the bird with softened butter and place it on a meat rack in a large roasting pan, breast side up. Sprinkle lightly with salt and pepper and dust lightly with flour.

Place it in the oven and after ¾ of an hour add 1 cup of stock to the pan. Cook for another hour and baste with the pan juices. Sprinkle again with salt and pepper and dust once more with flour. Reduce the oven heat to 325° F. and cook 2 hours and 15 minutes longer. Add more stock to the pan as needed and baste frequently. If for some reason or other the turkey is becoming too dark, put 2 thicknesses of waxed paper over the breast. At the end of the cooking time, prick the thighs to test for tenderness. Cut the strings and pull out both skewers. Test the legs again—if they move freely, the bird is cooked. Keep it warm on a serving platter or carving board while you make the sauce.

For the sauce, pour off as much of the pan fat as possible. Add 1 cup of strained stock and scrape the bottom and sides of the pan with a wooden spoon to dislodge the brown bits. Put the pan over moderate heat, add another cup of stock and cook, stirring occasionally, until there are about 1½ cups of liquid in the pan. Strain into a sauceboat. Taste the sauce and if it is too strong, dilute it with more stock. I doubt if more salt will be needed.

To carve the turkey, cut off the legs and divide them into drumstick and thigh. Remove the bone from each thigh and carve in thin slices—in this way everyone will get some dark meat. Cut off both wings, then carve the turkey in thin slices from top to bottom—breast to back—starting at the neck end.

Carrots, Turnips, and Green Beans

>   12 carrots
>   6 white turnips
>   2 lbs. green beans
>   2 Tbsp. salt
>   4 Tbsp. butter
>   Freshly ground black pepper
>   2 Tbsp. chopped parsley

Wash and scrape the carrots and cut them in 1½-inch pieces on the bias. Quarter the turnips; if they are large, cut them in eighths. Peel, making sure all the tough outside skin is removed, and shape slightly by cutting off the thin edge of the triangle. Cut off the tops and tails of beans and discard any with blemishes.

Bring 3 quarts of water to a boil in a heavy pan. Add 2 Tbsp. salt and the carrots and cook for approximately 5 to 6 minutes from the time the water returns to a boil. They should be firm and slightly underdone. Lift them out with a slotted spoon and put them in a bowl of cold water.

Add the turnips to the same boiling water and cook for 6 minutes, testing them after 5. Put them in the bowl of water with the carrots.

Bring the water to a boil once again and add the beans. Cook for 4 minutes and test one—they should be decidedly crisp. Drain and rinse them under cold running water. Drain the carrots and turnips and leave them in a collander with the beans until they are needed.

To heat, melt the butter in a heavy pan over low heat and add the vegetables—if they are dry they will be more evenly coated by the butter. Heat gently, seasoning if necessary with salt and freshly ground black pepper. Sprinkle with the chopped parsley before serving.

Cranberry Chutney

>   2 oranges
>   ½ cup red currant jelly
>   ½ cup light port wine
>   1½ to 2 cups sugar
>   2 sticks cinnamon
>   ¼ tsp. whole allspice } Tied in cheesecloth
>   2 cups fresh cranberries, washed and picked over

Cut the peel of one of the oranges in fine strips and simmer them in a little water for 2 to 3 minutes, then drain and set them aside.

Combine in a saucepan the juice of both oranges, the red currant jelly, port wine, sugar and cinnamon and allspice tied in cheesecloth. Bring to a boil and simmer for 5 minutes, then remove the spices and add the cranberries and the orange peel. Bring to a full rolling boil until the berries pop.

Cool, then store the chutney in glass jars until it's needed—it will keep almost indefinitely if properly sealed in sterilized jars. If you don't want to bother with this, it will keep for a good while in a container in the refrigerator.

Potato Purée

>   8 to 10 boiling potatoes
>   4 Tbsp. butter
>   ⅓ cup hot milk or cream
>   Salt and freshly ground black pepper
>   4 Tbsp. chives or parsley, finely chopped

Peel the potatoes and cut them in quarters to speed their cooking. Cover them with cold water in a heavy pan, adding 1 Tbsp. salt for each quart of water. Bring them to a boil and cook until tender—cooking time will vary from 20 to 40 minutes.

Drain them and place a folded towel over the pot for 5 minutes—the towel will absorb the excess steam. Put them through a food mill or use a masher or an electric mixer. Add 4 Tbsp. butter and approximately ⅓ cup of hot milk or cream to make a purée that is reasonably firm. Add salt and pepper to taste and the 4 Tbsp. of finely chopped chives or parsley.

Pumpkin Mousse

> 1 medium pumpkin, providing 2½ cups cooked pumpkin purée
> 2 Tbsp. gelatin
> ½ cup water
> 6 large eggs, separated
> 1 cup sugar
> ½ tsp. salt
> 1 cup milk
> ½ tsp. nutmeg
> ½ tsp. cinnamon
> ¼ cup brandy or rum
> 1 cup heavy cream, whipped with ¼ cup superfine sugar
> 6-cup soufflé dish

To prepare the pumpkin purée, cut the pumpkin in half and remove the seeds and threads. Bake it in a 325° oven for an hour until it's tender, then scrape the meat out of the shell. Force it through a wire strainer or ricer and beat it until smooth in an electric mixer or by hand with a sturdy wire whisk.

Fold a piece of heavy foil, long enough to encircle the soufflé dish, in half. Oil what will be the inside lightly, then tie it securely around the dish so that it stands 3 inches above its edge. Put it in the refrigerator until it is needed.

Sprinkle the gelatin over the ½ cup water and leave it to soften. Beat the egg yolks with the sugar until they are light and yellow. Heat the milk but do not boil and stir it into the egg yolks. In a large heavy pan combine the egg yolk mixture, pumpkin purée, salt and spices and cook carefully, stirring all the time, until it has thickened. Add the softened gelatin and stir until it's dissolved. Stir in the rum or brandy and add more sugar if you think it is needed. Cool the mixture.

When the mixture begins to set, and not before, beat the egg whites until they hold stiff peaks. Fold them lightly into the pumpkin mixture and spoon into the prepared soufflé dish. The mixture should come well above the rim of the dish. Chill in the refrigerator for at least 4 hours and decorate with the whipped cream, using a pastry bag and a rose tube to make 6 or 8 rosettes on top of the soufflé. Carefully remove the collar before bringing the soufflé to the table, and serve the remaining whipped cream separately.

Fruits and Nuts

Yellow and red apples arranged with black and green grapes, pears and tangerines will make an attractive, warm and seasonal display on the table.

After the traditional pumpkin there should be dishes of walnuts, filberts and pecans to be eaten with glasses of port.

❧ THE YEAR'S END ❧

It is my good fortune to like both Christmas and the last days of the year which have, for me, always been a time of great importance. I struggle to keep away from the commercial side of the festival, an effort that requires a will of iron. I avoid the spate of parties given at this time of year and ease myself into a mood of peace and quiet and hope that it will be sustained until the first day of the New Year. By then I have had time to entertain my friends at home and to have open house for those who are alone on Christmas Eve.

Christmas Eve is tailored to suit the taste of the very mixed group that comes to my house during the evening. Food en buffet is available from seven o'clock on for those who have finished last-minute shopping or who simply wish to make an appearance and exchange good wishes; others arrive late and go on to Midnight Mass. The planning will have been done a week beforehand, and there will be a variety of dishes on the buffet to cater to the varied tastes of my guests: striped bass is a favorite with those who prefer to eat lightly, and glazed corned beef ro those who need heartier fare. There should be little to do on the day itself but assemble the dishes for the buffet in the late afternoon and prepare oneself for a warm evening of very casual hospitality.

I rarely have a luncheon or dinner party on Christmas day if I have already entertained the evening before. But if I must have guests for both days, the Christmas day menu would not give me cause for worry. It has been chosen so that, once again, most of the work is done ahead of time. It should be a meal shared with friends in an atmosphere of peace, for which one is prepared to sit at the table for very much longer than usual, maybe with a glass of vintage port.

The ushering in of the New Year has undergone considerable transformation from the days of my youth. Instead of hunting, drinking and dancing into the small hours, then perhaps getting an hour's sleep before setting out for another hard day's hunting, I now find that I want to celebrate with a few old friends. I generally ask them to come at ten o'clock and serve supper at a quarter past eleven. Caviar and blini are served with iced vodka before going to the table, where we have my most favorite of soufflés—mushroom. Champagne is served with the soufflé, making sure there is enough to toast the birth of a New Year.

CHRISTMAS EVE BUFFET

Carriage House Terrine
Stuffed Striped Bass and Sauce Verte
Glazed Corned Beef
Potato Salad   Cheese
Praline Mousse   Mince Pies
Fresh Fruits

Serves 14 to 18

At first sight the menu for Christmas Eve looks formidable. But if you will give it some thought, you will see that most of it can be prepared well ahead of time, leaving little to do at the last minute except to arrange the buffet and set up a table for glasses and drinks.

The terrine may be made up to seven days beforehand. You will need to order the pork liver from a butcher well in advance, as it is not usually included in his everyday stock. An obliging butcher will grind the liver, fat belly and veal for you, thus saving you the greater part of the preparation. After it is cooked and cooled, pour clarified butter or melted lard over the terrine to keep out the air and it will come to no harm. However, I don't recommend freezing patés and terrines or in fact any pork products. I always make two terrines, as I can see no point in getting out the necessary equipment for one when little more time is needed for two. If you don't have a use for the second terrine, you may take my word for it that it makes a most acceptable gift at this time of year.

Choose the striped bass the day before Christmas Eve, if possible. Look for one with a bright and rather bulbous eye, scales that glisten and a sweet smell when you open one of the gills and put your nose close to it. A fish with a fishy smell and a dull, glazed eye should be avoided.

Make the stuffing in the morning and sew it into the fish later in the day. Bake it in the late afternoon but don't refrigerate it.

The Sauce Verte may be made two or three days ahead or whenever you have time. In fact, it is better made in advance if you can't find fresh tarragon in order to allow the dried herb to give up its full flavor.

The corned beef may be cooked two to three days beforehand if you have refrigerator space for it, and glazed the evening before Christmas Eve while you are making the potato salad. And remember to serve the potato salad at room temperature—if it has to be refrigerated, take it out an hour or two before it is to be served.

171

The cheeses of course must also be allowed to mellow at room temperature. I would suggest serving Brie, Fontina and Port de Salut or perhaps a Stilton or Gorgonzola, together with lots of good, crusty French bread.

The mousse can be made a week or two ahead and kept in the freezer. I would suggest taking individual ones out of the freezer as they are needed rather than running the risk of having several dissolve.

The mince pies (a term I willingly apply to these square or diamond-shaped pastries) keep extraordinarily well and may be frozen, but because of their richness need extra time out of the refrigerator or freezer to develop their full flavor.

The fruits may be arranged at any time during the day. Polish the apples and pears and wash the grapes. I sometimes arrange the hard fruits in compotes and put the grapes in a glass bowl with cracked ice.

It should now be obvious that this unwieldy-looking menu can quite comfortably be prepared in easy stages.

Carriage House Terrine

    2 lbs. fat belly of pork
    1 lb. pork liver
    1 lb. lean veal
    ½ lb. flare or fat back (sometimes called salt pork)
    1 clove garlic
    1 Tbsp. coarse salt
    12 black peppercorns
    12 juniper berries
    ½ tsp. mace
    1 cup white wine
    4 Tbsp. brandy
    Boiling water

Heat the oven to 325° F.

Grind together or chop very finely by hand the fat belly, pork liver and lean veal. Cut half the fat back in strips, then dice it coarsely and irregularly. Mix all these together in a porcelain bowl.

Peel and crush the garlic clove with 1 Tbsp. coarse salt. Crush the peppercorns and juniper berries, then add the garlic, peppercorns, juniper and the mace to the pork mixture. Pour the wine and brandy over all this, mix well and allow it to stand for 2 hours.

Cook 2 or 3 tablespoons of the mixture in a skillet for 5 or 6 minutes in order to taste it for seasoning and correct the terrine's seasoning accordingly by adding more salt and freshly ground black pepper if necessary. Pile the mixture into a 1-quart terrine or loaf pan. Cut the remaining fat back into thin strips and make a lattice pattern on the top.

Stand the terrine in a roasting pan, adding enough boiling water to come halfway up its sides. Cook it for 1½ hours, then allow it to cool. If it is to be kept longer than 4 or 5 days, pour melted clarified butter or lard on top to seal.

Stuffed Striped Bass and Sauce Verte

    1 striped bass (about 10 lbs.), cleaned
    5 eggs
    ½ tsp. salt
    ¼ tsp. pepper
    1 Tbsp. finely chopped parsley
    ½ Tbsp. finely chopped chives
    ¼ tsp. dried dill
    2 Tbsp. unsalted butter
    1 cup chopped shallots or scallions
    2 cups dry white wine
    Salt and pepper to taste

Sauce Verte:

    1 small bunch watercress
    2 packed cups parsley
    2 small bunches fresh tarragon (or
       1 Tbsp. dried tarragon)
    1 pint mayonnaise (½ the recipe given on page 99)
    2 Tbsp. lemon juice
    White pepper (optional)

Heat the oven to 400° F.

Wash the cleaned bass under running water, drain it and pat dry. Break the eggs into a mixing bowl, beat them lightly and add the salt, pepper, parsley, chives and dill. Melt the butter in a heavy skillet. Pour in the egg mixture and stir over low heat with a fork until it is cooked but not dry.

Stuff the bass with the egg mixture and sew up the opening. Oil a baking dish and make a bed of the shallots or scallions. Pour the wine over them and place the bass on top. Dust it lightly with salt and pepper and bake it for 35 to 40 minutes, basting frequently with the pan juices.

Meanwhile, to make the sauce, trim, wash and drain well the watercress, parsley and tarragon. Combine them with the mayonnaise in the blender and mix at full speed. Add the lemon juice and, if desired, the white pepper.

When the bass has finished cooking, remove it to a serving platter and serve at room temperature with the Sauce Verte.

Glazed Corned Beef

> 1 4- to 6-lb. corned beef
> Pot with lid large enough to hold the piece of beef
> Boiling water
> Whole cloves

Glaze:

> 1 small can crushed pineapple
> ½ cup orange marmalade
> 4 heaping Tbsp. domestic prepared mustard
> ¼ cup chopped candied cherries

Wash the corned beef under cold running water to remove any surface brine. Put the beef in the pot and cover it with boiling water, then simmer it for 3 to 4 hours with the lid on. When done, it should be easy to shove a fork through to the center. Take the cooked beef out of its pot and force it into a smaller one, putting a weight on it to compress it for easier slicing.

Meanwhile, to make the glaze, combine all the ingredients for it in a small, heavy pan and cook over medium heat until it's thickened.

Heat the oven to 450° F.

Put the corned beef on a greased baking sheet (one with an edge). Stud it with a pattern of cloves, then brush it with the glaze and bake for an hour, or until lightly browned, basting frequently and adding more glaze as necessary. Remove it to a serving platter and allow it to reach room temperature before serving.

Potato Salad

    4 lbs. small red round potatoes
    Salt
    2 mixings vinaigrette dressing (page 23)
    ¼ cup chopped parsley
    ¼ cup chopped chives
    1 Tbsp. capers, drained and chopped
    ¼ cup green onions, chopped
    Freshly ground black pepper
    Sprigs of parsley

Boil the potatoes in salted water, with 1 Tbsp. salt to every quart of water. Cook until tender, but take great care not to overcook them—they should be firm. When cool enough to handle, peel and slice the potatoes in ¼-inch slices.

Heat the vinaigrette dressing gently. Pour it over the still warm potatoes and mix carefully. Allow to soak until half an hour before serving.

Stir in the chopped herbs, capers and onions and season with freshly ground black pepper, if you think it is needed. Pile the salad in a serving bowl and garnish it with parsley sprigs.

The cheese, discussed in the introductory notes, should be taken out of the refrigerator in plenty of time to warm up to full flavor.

Praline Mousse

    3 eggs, separated
    ½ cup sugar
    2 Tbsp. Madeira
    6–8 Tbsp. praline powder
    2 cups heavy cream, chilled in the freezer for
       10 minutes before beating
    ¼ tsp. salt

Praline powder:

1 cup sugar
1 cup pecans, walnuts or filberts, toasted in the oven
1 cookie sheet, lightly oiled

To make the praline powder, dissolve or melt the sugar over low heat, preferably in a pan that is not much used, stirring constantly. Raise the heat and cook till brown—I like a dark amber in preference to a lighter color, but this is a matter of taste; some find the darker syrup makes a bitter praline. As the syrup turns color add the toasted nuts and stir to coat evenly. When it has reached the desired color pour it in an even stream onto the oiled cookie sheet. Allow it to harden and cool. When quite hard and cold, break it off the sheet by bending the sheet—it will come away quite easily. Grind it to a coarse powder with a bottle or rolling pin; if you own a blender the operation will only take seconds. Store the praline in a screw-top jar in the refrigerator until you're ready to use it.

To make the mousse, beat the egg yolks with the ½ cup of sugar until light in color and creamy. Mix in the Madeira and praline powder. Beat the chilled cream until soft peaks are formed, and fold it carefully into the egg-yolk mixture.

Beat the egg whites with the salt until definite peaks are formed. Spoon two large spoonfuls of the beaten egg white into the egg-cream mixture, mix to lighten it and then fold in the remainder of the egg whites. Spoon into ramekins that hold ¾ cup and freeze.

When frozen the ramekins should be wrapped in a plastic wrap to seal. They may be stored almost indefinitely in the freezer. Remove from the freezer about 10 minutes before serving and sprinkle the tops with a little praline powder.

Mince Pies

> 2 recipes short pastry (page 72)
> 2 14–15 oz. jars of mincemeat
> ½ cup dark rum
> 2 egg yolks beaten well with ⅓ cup heavy cream
> Superfine sugar

Heat the oven to 375° F.

Butter, then line a 15¾- x 10½-inch baking sheet with an edge with half the short pastry rolled out to a thickness of approximately one-eighth of an inch allowing about half an inch to hang over the edge all the way around. Bake for 10 minutes.

Mix the 2 jars of mincemeat with the rum and spread the mixture evenly over the pastry-lined baking sheet. Roll out the remaining pastry and cover the mincemeat, pinching together carefully the unbaked and half-baked pastry edges. Brush the top with the egg yolk and cream, then with a sharp knife score the pastry in squares or diamond shapes in the size you want to serve it, being careful not to cut through the pastry.

Bake for 15 to 20 minutes in the 375° oven, being careful not to let the top get too brown. Dust with superfine sugar as soon as it comes out of the oven, and allow to cool slightly before breaking into the pieces you have marked.

CHRISTMAS DAY DINNER

Double Tomato Consommé
Capon Demi Désossée
Purée of Broccoli
Plum Pudding
Hard Sauce
Fruit Compote

Serves 8 to 10

Soups have a tendency to improve with keeping and the stock which will be the base for the tomato consommé freezes like a dream. Finish the consommé on Christmas morning and correct the seasoning after it has been heated. Avoid bringing it to a boil the second time.

Bone the capon exactly according to the instructions for the Thanksgiving turkey. Chill it and the stuffing before assembling it—I prefer to do this in the morning of the day it is to be cooked.

The purée of broccoli can be prepared well ahead of time. Pour a little melted butter over the surface to keep air out and to prevent its darkening. Reheat gently and correct the seasoning before serving.

When making the compote, as always peel and slice the citrus fruits first, working over a bowl so that all the juices are caught. You can now safely add the apples and pears, as the acid in the citrus fruit juice prevents their turning brown. Be sure they are coated thoroughly with the juice before continuing your preparations.

Plum pudding virtually looks after itself once it's in the cooking pot, and the hard sauce to be served with it may be made the morning before Christmas and refrigerated.

Again, this is not an overpowering menu when the work is planned ahead to be done at your convenience.

Double Tomato Consommé

    2 quarts stock
    1 large can Italian tomatoes with basil
    ½ cup dry white vermouth
    ½ cup parsley sprigs
    Rind of 1 lemon
    Salt and pepper

Stock (2 quarts):

    6 13- or 14-oz. cans clear chicken broth
    1 boiling hen or the carcasses of 2 chickens with giblets
       but not livers, if your butcher can provide you with them
    2 ribs celery, chopped
    2 carrots, chopped
    1 medium onion, peeled and chopped
    6 peppercorns
    1 bay leaf
    2 Tbsp. coarse salt

To make the stock, put all its ingredients in a 6- to 8-quart pot, cover with cold water and bring to a boil. Lower the heat immediately and simmer very gently for 3 hours, adding water as necessary to keep its level just above the solids. If a gentle simmer is maintained it will not be necessary to clarify the stock. Strain it into a clean pot or bowl and let it cool. When it's cold, remove all the fat from the surface.

Bring the stock and tomatoes to a boil in a 4-quart pot. Strain through a medium strainer without crushing the tomato pulp too much—overcrushing tends to make the consommé cloudy. Add the vermouth and correct the seasoning with additional salt and pepper if necessary.

Just before serving, heat the consommé thoroughly and chop the parsley and lemon rind together, sprinkling a little over each serving as you spoon it out in the kitchen or at the table.

Capon Demi Désossée

    1 6-lb. capon, half-boned

Stuffing:

    2 chicken breasts (from 1 chicken), boned, and 1 lb. lean
       veal ground together
    6 oz. salt pork, diced small
    ¼ cup good brandy
    ½ cup dry white wine
    1 Tbsp. salt
    1 tsp. dried tarragon
    ½ tsp. freshly ground black pepper
    1 liver from the capon, finely chopped
    Pot with a lid just big enough to hold the capon,
       preferably enamel-coated or stainless steel
    1 bottle dry white wine for poaching

Sauce:

    4 cups strained stock, reduced to 2
    5 egg yolks
    1 cup heavy cream
    4 Tbsp. unsalted butter
    Finely chopped parsley for garnish

Partially bone the capon according to the instructions for the turkey on pages 160-161. Simmer the bones you remove in enough water to cover them in a small saucepan—this stock will be added to the wine for poaching, if needed.

Mix together all the ingredients for the stuffing and pile it into the capon's cavity; mound to the shape of a whole bird. Take 6 pieces of the capon's breast you laid aside in the process of half-boning, lay them over the mounded stuffing and bring the skin of the capon up to cover the mounded stuffing and breast meat in a natural-looking way. With a needle and string sew the two halves of the skin together, starting from the tail of the bird. Tie the capon firmly in a piece of doubled cheese cloth. It is now ready for the pot.

Place the capon breast side up in the pot, pouring the bottle of white wine over it. If there is not enough to cover ⅔ of the bird, add sufficient stock to do so. Bring to a boil on top of the stove, then lower the heat and simmer gently, covered, for an hour and a half. Test after an hour by moving the leg; if it moves freely, it is most likely done.

Apply a second test by sticking a sharp knife into the thigh or drumstick. If the juices run clear, the bird is cooked. Lift the capon from the pot very gently so as not to break it, and keep it warm while you strain the stock from the pot and finish the sauce.

Take 4 cups of stock in which the bird was cooked and boil them rapidly until you have 2. Beat the 5 egg yolks lightly and mix with the 1 cup of heavy cream. Stir into the warm stock and heat gently until it thickens. At the last minute stir in the 4 Tbsp. butter bit by bit and correct the seasoning.

Spoon some of the sauce over the capon and serve the remainder in a warmed sauceboat. Sprinkle the chopped parsley over the dish.

Purée of Broccoli

> 4 bundles of broccoli
> 2 Tbsp. salt
> Cheesecloth
> 4 Tbsp. butter, softened
> 1 cup sour cream
> Freshly ground black pepper

Bring 3 to 4 quarts of water to a boil in a kettle.

Wash the broccoli, trim the stalks and remove the coarse outside bark with a vegetable peeler. Stand the broccoli in a pot large enough to hold it, with the stalks down, and sprinkle it with the 2 Tbsp. salt (if you don't have a pot large enough to hold all the broccoli, cook it in 2 pots). Pour enough of the boiling water over the broccoli to cover the stalks, but don't submerge the heads.

Cover with the dampened cheesecloth, bring to a boil over high heat and cook for 6 minutes. The steam trapped by the cheesecloth will cook the broccoli tops. Drain and chop coarsely, then purée in a blender, adding the butter and sour cream to assist in the blending. Season the purée with freshly ground black pepper and with more salt, if needed, and serve it hot.

Plum Pudding

    1¾ lbs. beef suet
    1   lb. white bread crumbs from stale bread
    ¾   lb. raisins (large)
    ¾   lb. currants
    ¾   lb. sultanas (yellow raisins)
    4   cups all-purpose flour
    1   tsp. baking powder
    8   large eggs
    ½   cup brandy
    2   24-inch squares of clean cloth
    ¼   cup brandy for flaming

Chill the beef suet thoroughly. Remove the membrane and grate it on the coarsest side of your grater. Prepare the bread crumbs from stale bread, and wash and dry the currants, raisins and sultanas. Sift the flour and baking powder together, then mix all the dry ingredients in a large bowl. Beat the eggs lightly and add the ½ cup brandy to them, then pour into the bowl with the dry ingredients and mix thoroughly.

Have ready two 24-inch squares of clean cloth. Flour each generously and pile half of the pudding on each piece of cloth. Gather up the edges and tie them securely with heavy string. Bring to a boil a pot of water large enough to hold both, or a pot for each, and boil for 5 hours. The pudding may now be drained and hung up by its string. It will keep in this way for a year.

To serve the pudding, boil for 1 hour and unwrap from its cloth on a serving dish. It is usual to pour warm brandy over it and bring it to the table in flames with a sprig of holly stuck in the top.

Serve with hard sauce.

Hard Sauce

> 2 cups confectioner's sugar
> 8 Tbsp. unsalted butter, softened
> 3 Tbsp. brandy
> ¼ cup heavy cream

Add the sugar gradually to the softened butter, using an electric beater or a large electric mixer, if you have one. Mix until well blended. Add the brandy and mix again, then beat in the ¼ cup heavy cream.

Chill thoroughly to serve.

Fruit Compote

> 4 dessert oranges
> 1 grapefruit
> Small bunch green seedless grapes
> Small bunch black grapes
> 2 Yellow Delicious apples
> 2 pears, not overripe
> 1 small ripened pineapple
> 2 bananas
> Superfine sugar (optional)

Over a mixing bowl, peel and slice the oranges into segments, cutting between the membrane and the flesh to release each pith-free segment and catching the juices in the bowl. Squeeze what's left to get all of the juice. Treat the grapefruit in the same way.

Cut the seedless grapes in half and add them to the fruit in the bowl. Cut the black grapes in half and remove the seeds, then add them to the other fruits. Peel and core the apples and pears, then quarter them and slice thinly. Mix them well with the citrus fruit and grapes to coat them with the juices.

Peel and core the pineapple and cut it into bite-size pieces, adding them to the bowl. Chill until needed.

Before serving, peel and slice the bananas and mix with the other fruit. Add superfine sugar to taste, if needed, and serve cold in a glass dish.

NEW YEAR'S EVE SUPPER

Blini with Caviar
Sour Cream
Mushroom Soufflé
Salad Paulette
Coffee Parfait

Serves 6 to 8

This meal gives me a feeling of once-a-year extravagance appropriate to the occasion. Unlike most of my menus, it requires that you spend time in the kitchen (unless you are in the fortunate position of having someone else do the cooking), since blini do not reheat well and must be eaten as soon as they are cooked. If you are concerned about deserting your guests, ask them to join you in the kitchen—they may look on at the proceedings with considerable interest. I encourage my guests to drink champagne or ice-cold Russian vodka as the appropriate accompaniments to the menu, but they are of course welcome to their choice of liquor.

The batter for the blini requires five to six hours to rise properly, and so must be made well in advance. Prepare the caviar tray early in the evening, putting out on it small plates, knives or spreaders, plenty of napkins, spoons for the caviar and sour cream and a dish for lemon wedges. A bowl of cracked ice large enough to hold the caviar can be kept in the freezer and brought out at the last minute.

Make the mushroom soufflé base early on—it may be prepared in the morning if you wish. Have the egg whites ready for beating and the oven at the right temperature. You will find that little more than five minutes will be needed to put the soufflé together, and your guests will scarcely miss you if they are still occupied with the blini or with a drink. Be emphatic about having them at the table five minutes before the soufflé is ready to come out of the oven. They will then have to wait for it, not the other way round.

The salad can be dressed just before you expect your guests, as it is fairly sturdy and will stand the test of time better than delicate green leaves. The coffee parfait should hopefully have been made days before so that you need only remember to take it out of the freezer and put it in the refrigerator twenty minutes before serving.

189

Blini with Caviar

    2 to 2¼ cups milk
    1 package dry yeast or 1 cake compressed yeast
    ½ cup warm water
    1 cup flour
    1½ cups buckwheat flour
    ½ tsp. salt
    3 eggs, separated
    3 Tbsp. melted butter
    3 Tbsp. sour cream
    8 oz. caviar or as much as you can afford
    Bowl of sour cream (about 1 pint)

Bring the milk to a boil and cool it to lukewarm. Sprinkle the yeast over the ½ cup warm water and let it stand for 5 minutes. Meanwhile, sift the flour with half the buckwheat flour (¾ cup) and the salt into a bowl. Make a well in the center and add the softened yeast mixture with 1 cup of the lukewarm milk. Stir gradually drawing in the flour to make a smooth batter, then beat well for 2 minutes. (This may be done with less labor in the bowl of a mixer, using a dough hook or paddle.) Cover the bowl with a damp cloth and let it rise in a warm place for 2 to 3 hours or until the batter is light and full of bubbles. Then beat the mixture to knock out the air and beat in the remaining ¾ cup buckwheat flour. Cover and allow to rise again until the batter is doubled in bulk, about 2 hours.

Beat in the second cup of milk until the batter is smooth, then beat in the egg yolks, melted butter and sour cream, and a little more milk, if necessary—the batter should be the consistency of heavy cream. Beat the egg whites until they hold a stiff peak, then fold them into the batter and let stand for 30 minutes.

Heat a lightly buttered griddle or heavy skillet and pour in the batter with a small ladle to make 3-inch rounds. Cook for 2 to 3 minutes until the undersides of the blini are slightly browned and the tops are bubbling, then turn them and brown the other side. Keep the blini warm while cooking the rest of the batter and serve them hot. They do not reheat well.

To eat them, brush the blini with salted butter, add a spoonful of sour cream and top with caviar, and use your fingers rather than a fork.

Mushroom Soufflé

½ lb. mushrooms
5 Tbsp. butter
5 Tbsp. flour
1 tsp. salt
¼ tsp. paprika
Dash of cayenne pepper
1½ cups hot milk
¾ cup Parmesan cheese, grated
6 egg yolks
8 egg whites
Pinch of cream of tartar

Heat the oven to 400° F.

Wipe the mushrooms with a damp cloth and slice them thinly. Melt the butter in a heavy pan and add the flour, salt, paprika and cayenne. Cook for 3 minutes, stirring. Heat the milk to just under a boil and add it gradually to the roux, whisking vigorously. Add the Parmesan.

Separate the eggs and add the yolks and the mushrooms to the roux. Beat the 8 egg whites and the cream of tartar until stiff, then fold them into the mixture. Pour gently into a 2-quart greased soufflé dish. Mark a smaller circle on top of the soufflé with a knife to enable it to rise like a hat. Bake for 35 minutes. Always serve soufflé from the center, not from the outer edge.

Salad Paulette

4 ribs celery
2 lbs. fresh green beans
2 Tbsp. salt
6 to 8 small red potatoes
1 small can truffles
1 cup commercial mayonnaise
1 mixing vinaigrette dressing (page 23)
½ cup parsley sprigs, finely chopped
Salt and pepper

Wash the ribs of celery and remove any tough outer skin with a vegetable peeler. Slice very thinly on the bias. Wash the beans and cut off the tops and tails. Bring 2 quarts of water to a boil and add 2 Tbsp. salt. Add the beans and cook for 4 minutes after the water comes to the boil again, or al dente—test one with your teeth. Lift them out and run cold water over them, then allow them to dry first in a collander and then on paper towels. Discard any that are too thick or long.

Boil the potatoes, unpeeled, in the water you used for the beans, until tender, then drain and dry them thoroughly and cut into small dice.

Drain the truffles and slice very thinly. Slice again in matchsticks.

Thin the mayonnaise with the vinaigrette dressing to the consistency of heavy cream. Put all the vegetables and most of the chopped parsley in a large bowl. Mix with the prepared dressing, taking great care not to add too much—the julienne of vegetables should be well-coated and no more—and season with salt and pepper to taste. Spoon into the salad bowl—a glass one is ideal—and sprinkle the remaining parsley on top before serving.

Coffee Parfait

¾ cup of sugar
⅓ cup of water
4 egg yolks
Dash of salt
2 cups heavy cream
2 Tbsp. powdered instant coffee
2 tsp. vanilla
1-oz. square bitter chocolate, shaved with a heavy knife

Boil the sugar and water in a saucepan until the syrup spins a thread, 230° on a candy thermometer. Or put some syrup on the thumb of one hand with a spoon, then close the thumb and first finger. If when they are separated the syrup forms a thread, it has reached the right temperature. Meanwhile, beat the egg yolks and salt together thoroughly. Beat the hot syrup into the egg yolks in a thin stream, add instant coffee and continue beating until cool. Beat together the heavy cream and vanilla until the cream holds definite peaks. Fold this into the yolk mixture, along with some of the chocolate shavings, reserving the rest for a garnish.

Spoon into ⅓-cup ramekins and freeze until frim. The parfaits should be moved from the freezer to the refrigerator 20 minutes before serving to soften a bit, and decorated with chocolate shavings. I suggest you bring them out as needed to avoid letting them dissolve before they can be eaten.

❧ INDEX ❧